I0003788

Praise for The Principle of Relevance

We need to learn how to filter out unnecessary information and select and use what is relevant, the author provides tools to help readers achieve this
The South China Morning Post

Her way - the principle of relevance - is the key to convert information from a chaotic and shapeless mass into an instrument to empower ourselves, our capabilities and our ambitions, whatever they are, professional or private.....
In a very easy way, she drives us back to our purposes and the true meaning of our searches, pushing ahead a fundamental concept: whatever the focus of our search is on and whatever its purpose is, we must always start from ourselves and not from external data.
Maria Cristina Ferradini, *Director, Legal Department, Vodafone Italy*

If you often find yourself in information overload, this Principle, when mastered can change your life. As a logical, linear thinker, I had to laugh at how the author "pegged" my actions and the urgency of my distractions. Stefania provides tools to assist all of us in breaking the habits that keep us from being truly effective.
Judy Irving, *Executive Coach, Moving On, USA*

The book lives up to its name. To discover that it also excelled at offering practical, best practice advice was an absolute blessing. Navigating the streams of information that now cascade towards us is not realistic. With the aid of the ideas and solutions laid out in easy to follow steps, the readers will hone their "new media" instincts.
A fascinating and educational book.
Nick West, *Head of Conferences and Events, Financial Times, Asia Pacific*

As a former corporate director now in the consultation business, I have been perplexed about the issue of why our managers and employees are becoming more and more activities driven rather than results based. This book went to the very heart of my problem.....
Reader review, Amazon

Read this book and you might see the light on how to take the leap from mere professional to that of a superstar!"
Reader review, Amazon
The Principle of Relevance has become a practical tool to help me rethink how I was approaching my business. I think every entrepreneur should read it to understand the secret of focusing on relevance rather than reacting to a flood of inputs. A uniquely inspiring book!
Reader review, Amazon

I wish The Principle of Relevance had been written years ago, as it has been eye opening. Better than any "goal setting" course I have ever taken.

Reader review, Amazon

I highly recommend this book to anyone who is looking to get laser focused and increase their level of effectiveness and productivity.

Reader review, Barnes and Noble

The Principle of Relevance

The Essential Strategy to Navigate through the Information Age

Stefania Lucchetti

Originally published by

Restless Travellers (RT) Publishing

Hong Kong

ISBN 9798323192373

© 2009 Stefania Lucchetti

All rights reserved. No part of this publication may be photocopied or reproduced, stored in a retrieval system, or transmitted in any form or by any means, electronic, mechanical, recording, or otherwise, without the prior written permission of the author or the publisher.

First print: Hong Kong SAR, February 2010

Second print: Canada, February 2011

Third Print: Milano, April 2024

This book is dedicated to my very much missed grandmother, Carla.

There are roads not to take

There are armies not to attack

There are towns not to besiege

There are terrains not to contest

There are ruler's orders not to obey

Sun Tzu, *The Art of War*

CONTENTS

RELEVANCE TOOLS in PART II

Relevance Tool N. 1 – The Outcome Checklist
  (Relevance Tool N. 1 – Example)
Relevance Tool N. 2 – The Perception Chart: Recognizing Data Relevance
  (Relevance Tool N. 2 – Example)
Relevance Tool N. 3 – The Context Chart
  (Relevance Tool N. 3 – Example)
Relevance Tool N. 4 – The Baconian Pattern Chart
  (Relevance Tool N. 4 – Example)
Relevance Tool N. 5 – Traditional Mind Mapping
Relevance Tool N. 6 – Layered Mind Mapping
  (Relevance Tool N. 6 – Example)
Relevance Tool N. 7 – Multiple Players Mind Mapping
  (Relevance Tool N. 7 – Example)
Relevance Tool N. 8 – The Attention Exercise
  (Relevance Tool N. 8 – Example)

ACKNOWLEDGMENTS

Many people and experiences have, throughout the years, influenced the creation of this book and contributed to its development, though this limited space only allows a few to be mentioned.

I hold dear to my heart those whose love, cheer, and support have fuelled the strength, focus, and alchemist fire that enabled the transformation of an idea into a book.

To the numerous friends and acquaintances I had the privilege of sharing ideas and drafts with throughout the creative process and who gifted me with insightful comments and suggestions that helped alter the shape of the book for the better.

PREFACE

Much has passed since the first edition of The Principle of Relevance was first released in Hong Kong.

During these months, I have been speaking to corporate audiences, I have been teaching in universities, I have been speaking to schools.

The topics related to information overload that come up time and time again, that people want to discuss at length, are usually two.

The first is *emails*. At the moment, executives are haunted about the enormous quantity of e-mails they receive on a constant basis, on the computer and on their Blackberry. Most executives receive an average of 300 e-mails every day, as e-mail is currently used in the corporate world for any kind of communication, even when a quick exchange of live chats - or a conversation - would be more appropriate.

E-mail communications require structured thoughts. They are one-way communications, like letters, and therefore they are not practical for immediate, spontaneous, quick exchanges of thoughts. The misuse of emails creates situations where executives receive (and send) what I call "stream of consciousness" e-mails: one-liners of unstructured thought that create a lot of e-mail clutter without being productive.

The second topic, that haunts educators and parents is the form that *knowledge* is taking.

1

Knowledge is of two kinds: either we know a subject ourselves, or we know where we can find information on it.

The net opens access to an infinite library of easily and quickly retrievable information, accessible just by typing a few keywords. It functions as a sort of external hard drive, an outsourced memory we can plug in at any time.

Because of this, some have argued that the net dilutes the most traditional kind of knowledge: knowing a subject ourselves. It therefore makes our brains shallow, diminishing our intelligence and killing our inner memory.

But is this really true? Or should we evolve in our understanding of what brain power and memory are?

If you are in your thirties and forties, you probably remember that when you were a teenager you knew by heart the phone number of your closest friends. Since the introduction of digital directories, smartphones and services like plaxo there is no longer any reason to memorize numbers by heart. On the other hand, how many contacts do you have now compared to then thanks to the digital directories? How much more connected are you?

Yes, the information age allow us to know less, in terms of depth of what we know, as mentioned by David Brooks, a New York Times columnist, in his famous 2006 NY Times article "The Outsourced Brain."

The positive side of this is that we are free to expand our awareness of subjects we did not have space, or availability, to explore before. Our

2

memory now has a different function: it is an index, it remembers the existence of a subject and what are the best leads to find information on that subject.

You don't need to memorize the content of a book, you just need to be aware of the existence of a book. Although this might make your middle school English teacher cringe, it is time to stop identifying ourselves with our memory and start seeing it as a flexible tool of the brain, which does not necessarily need to be contained within the brain it serves.

Your outsourced memory – the net – allows you to be aware of the existence of information you would never have come across before when you were limited to what your inner memory could hold. It allows you to increase the quantity of information that you can process because you do not always have to worry about memorizing every single detail of it, and for this same reason it allows you to use more brain power in linking concepts and applying them rather than remembering them.

It therefore empowers you to think and process information faster because your brain has the space to hold links to so much different information, and in doing so it expands your subjective time.

Does this mean that the internet is transforming our brain into a copy of itself, like Nicholas Carr states in his 2010 book The Shallows? Yes, probably, but how is this necessarily a bad thing, a "shallowing" of our brain, or is it instead an expansion of our brain, a leap forward in our evolution if we learn to use this technology consciously? If we learn to use it to our advantage?

Back in the analogue era, the difference between a deep brain and a shallow brain was the availability of information and the choice of whether to take in that information or not came second. Now that everything is available, the power is back to you: it is up to you to take responsibility of what content goes into your mind and how you use your outsourced memory.

This is where this book comes in. The vision and purpose of *The Principle of Relevance* is to deepen your awareness of the complexities and opportunities offered by the current unfolding era and to give you, the reader, strategic tools that will empower you to be effective, through deliberate awareness building and choice of action. Choice about what to do and when; to observe, find, and pay attention to the data, events, things, and personal interactions that are of importance; and ultimately, to move on when a particular journey has come to an end.

I am confident that this book will satisfy all knowledge seekers. If you are philosophically inclined, you will find insights and thought triggers that will expand your holistic awareness. If you prefer practical readings, you will find specific tools and knowledge to sharpen the razor of your mind and focus.

INTRODUCTION

We live in a world where information is so readily available that wealth and time no longer constitute a barrier to knowledge and learning to anyone possessing a computer and an Internet connection.

Information creates stimuli, knowledge, and choices. And yet, the paradoxical consequence of data overload and an abundance of equally attractive choices is uncertainty of purpose. This uncertainty undermines resolution and focus, ultimately devaluing the very freedom that an abundance of choices unlocks. This factor has introduced a new level of complexity that reflects not only on our social structure, but also on our cognitive processes and on our ability to find meaning and purpose in the activities we pursue.

As the complexity of culture evolves and choices increase, it becomes increasingly difficult to achieve a degree of resolve as to what we should pay attention to and in which direction we should dedicate our energy and efforts. Our souls are in a state of confusion because of our inability to find meaning and purpose in a range of seemingly unlimited opportunities. As our choices increase, the questions that seem to press more and more on each one of us are "What should I pay attention to? What should I get involved with?".

Too many stimuli, goals, and events are competing for our attention, each one seeking prominence. We often feel lost as complexity and entropy seem constantly to increase.

We must cultivate our ability to work through the tangled bundle of conflicting inputs being addressed to us and choose to respond only to the ones that will give purpose to our actions. We must find a way to master our ability to surf through unlimited data and options and become skillful at making fast choices as to what is worth our time and our energy, because time and energy spent on something makes us who we ultimately become, our lives.

How do you train yourself to navigate through the information age, being able to take advantage of data, tools, and resources without being overwhelmed and swallowed by the seemingly unsustainable demand of data overflow? How do you become effective, rather than being simply efficient? How do you keep your competitive advantage when information is so freely available? How can you understand which information and tools are relevant to your goals and which are not? How do you navigate through increasingly complex interactions?

This is the journey through which this book intends to guide you.

PART I

THE PRINCIPLE OF RELEVANCE

Anything less than a conscious commitment to the important is an

unconscious commitment to the unimportant.

Stephen Covey, *The 7 Habits of Highly Effective People*

The Principle of Relevance

ONE

The Principle of Relevance Discovered

1.   Everyday Experiences

Though not everyone works in a corporate office, an ordinary day in the life of the average office worker – let us call him (or her) Chris - can illustrate the issues we will be discussing.

Chris wakes up in the morning and goes through the ordinary morning routine: washes, has breakfast, possibly goes to the gym if he is a morning person, then drives or takes public transport to the office. He arrives at the office and opens his computer; perhaps, if he has time, he scrolls through today's paper or, more likely, the daily e-news digest, then starts working on the project or assignment that he has chosen to dedicate his energies to throughout that day, or that his supervisors or his clients have asked him to address.

Does this sound familiar? It seems to describe the average day of most people who have an office job. And yet, if you can relate to this narrative, you may feel that your own typical day involves much more than this skeletal, simplistic, almost ideal description.

Let's try again.

Chris wakes up in the morning, and the first thing he does is check his BlackBerry. He has around thirty or more new e-mails: overseas clients

9

and business partners have been working throughout his night and have processed a number of issues on which they need feedback.

The mobile Facebook application also flashes with a couple new messages and friends invites. Outlook reminds him that a client lunch and a meeting at ten are scheduled for today. He takes care of all the e-mails, responding to each one, then rushes through his routine, has breakfast, and goes to work. Typically, he either arrives at work late, or the time spent answering those thirty e-mails will have robbed him of the time to read the paper or have a chat with his spouse. By the time he gets to the office, at least half the people copied in the thirty e-mails to which he has responded will have replied back with their thoughts. Three or four people are copied in one e-mail, so he receives sixty e-mails back. Most of the replies don't add any new information, insight, or instruction; rather, they just expand on previous e-mails in a disorganized, entropic way. However, as soon as Chris opens his computer, he feels compelled to reply right away. Never mind that replying takes another sixty minutes and prevents him from kicking off on the actual work he has planned to do that day.

By mid-morning, Chris is running late on his schedule, but he still feels that he will be able to deliver his analysis by lunchtime. Chris's boss walks in and tells him that there is an urgent issue that requires immediate attention. Chris points out that the analysis needs to be delivered by lunchtime today, but the look on his boss's face tells him that he doesn't appreciate being pushed back.

He feels that the issue Chris's supervisor wants him to deal with, although related to the main project and even relatively important, could easily and quickly be dealt with once the analysis is finished as the outcome of the analysis would point out a direction and a solution to a number of related minor issues. Yet, the client is pressing for an immediate answer, and the supervisor is not the kind of person to negotiate. Chris has to stop his analysis, prepare an answer for the client, and answer another round of about ten e-mails back and forth; by the time this is over, it is four o'clock.

The deadline for delivery of the analysis is postponed until tomorrow, and though on one hand, Chris is relieved, on the other hand, he knows this means that another minor problem of a similar sort will urgently be placed on his desk tomorrow morning. Chris commits to getting the analysis done during the night, no matter what it takes, so as to avoid other useless delays. However, his spouse calls him to remind him that he has promised to get involved in organizing their next vacation, so he gets on Google to search for flights, hotels, and relevant information. There are about four official Web sites, ten travel agencies, and an undetermined number of various random information Web sites, including blogs, podcasts, and dedicated content pages. He decides to travel the old route and just buy a guide from the online bookstore, but the Web site presents three options: hardcopy, e-book, and audiobook.

It takes Chris a half hour to browse through the different options, fill out the order form, retrieve his PayPal password, and place an order for the hardcopy version. By the time he has finished, it is eight o'clock. He hasn't organized the trip, he hasn't delivered the analysis, and he is late for dinner: he is aware of that because his mobile phone keeps ringing and shows five unread text messages.

Chris feels that he has accomplished little and that for some reason, powers beyond his control have eaten up all his time.

Does this sound a bit more familiar?

Some time ago in my practice as a corporate attorney I was working on a business deal – one of the painful ones where a huge team is called to work 24/7 to produce a result in record time. There was a lot of work to be carried out, everyone was stressed by the long working hours and the deadlines. And yet, something mystifying (and hilarious, if it hadn't been so frustrating) was happening: notwithstanding the fact that everyone was supposed to be working away at documents and analysis, we all would be submersed – literally – with a flood of incessant emails, sometime more than one per minute. Someone would send some information, question or comment – most of the times about an infinitesimally small and sometimes irrelevant issue compared to the big picture we were aiming to draw together – to a whole list of addressees and everyone would answer with their comment, and so on. If a comment, often unnecessary, was not provided within a short period of time, someone would prompt for it. As a result, I – like most others – spent all my time reading emails and responding to them as they came, and not having the time to perform what had to be my actual job until very late at night. Most of these email interactions, as it often is, turned out to be superfluous and unnecessary at the end of the day when, having finally been able to carry out the analysis that was required, we had all our answers and someone was able to put together a thought through summary. How much faster, better and effectively would we have worked if we had been able to control that impatient email flow.

12

2. The Information Age

In its infancy, the information age expanded the ability of individuals to both access and transfer information, therefore gaining admittance to knowledge that previously would have been difficult to find. The Web and its derivative tools (like e-mail communications) were mainly information highways, enabling the delivery of information and mainly functioning on the basis of an individual, one-to-one relationship. An individual would access information included on a particular Web site or in the contents of an e-mail.

The information age has evolved into a new life phase in the last decade, thanks to the second generation of Web development and Web design tools and the way in which these tools are being used, commonly known as *Web 2.0.* The new generation of information-sharing technical tools (such as "wikis") and the new commercial enterprises they have generated (e.g., social networking sites like Facebook or Twitter and media-sharing sites like YouTube) have led to the development and evolution of Web-based communities, hosted services, and Web applications.

The mature stage of the information age in which we are currently living is no longer about accessing and transferring information, but rather about networking, real-time information updating, and real-time peer input, which has changed the very nature of information itself. Don Tapscott and

Anthony D. Williams, in their book *Wikinomics*,[1] analyze in great detail the paradigm shift set in motion in offline life by the philosophy of peer cooperation underlying Web 2.0—not only in social networking, but also in the business world. Business models formerly based on hierarchical power structures and the use of internal resources have been forced to change into "peering" models, based on horizontal organization, self-organization, and information-based cooperation projects. A quintessential example of this transformation is the revolution brought about in the software industry with the development and introduction of Linux. It is obvious how this radical evolution in information sharing has facilitated the creation, consumption, and manipulation of knowledge.

Virtually any bit of knowledge on whatever topic the mind can imagine can be retrieved, starting off from a simple search on Google and skillfully following its thread, and the three-dimensional nature of Web 2.0 applications offers as many perspectives on a given topic as one would like. We have finally come to a time in which wealth, time, and resources no longer constitute a barrier to knowledge and learning.

3. Digital Information

The whole concept of what it means to develop information has changed before our eyes in a very short period of time: we grew up in a time when information was something material, physical, a "thing" that could be found in a logical place (e.g., a library shelf, an office archive, or

---

[1] Don Tapscott and Anthony D. Williams, *Wikinomics* (Portfolio, 2008).

a file system organized according to logical, hierarchical categories). We have journeyed through our school years thinking that information would require expert knowledge to be produced and managed, and that it would require much effort to find and understand.

It is obvious now that these assumptions only applied when information was produced and managed on paper. Digital information is so different that it requires a radical rethinking beyond our usual concepts of form. Digital information takes different forms, or sometimes does not have a definite material form, a support, and a mechanical container. Digital information is not organized in a hierarchical way. Just take a moment to visualize or think conceptually about the World Wide Web: there is no top to the Web, no center; you can look at it from different points of observation, and you will have the same view. Any page on the Web will be interlinked to other pages in a nonhierarchical way and from whatever angle at which you view it. In the digital information age, there are no shelves, no categories; there is no logical place where information can be found, and yet information can be found everywhere.

Any book or piece of information can be tagged into a system and therefore stored in a number of places at once, without restricted, closed, bound categories, and without limits. This allows each one of us to stretch beyond material constraints and reach information that would have been unreachable before, while at the same time, it stretches and challenges our mental and physical boundaries, our sense of space, forcing us to think beyond the three dimensions of our physical world.

In a couple of decades, thanks to nanotechnology, knowledge will dominate the economy. Nanotechnology, the intersection of information and the physical world, promises the tools to rebuild the physical world, our bodies and brains included, molecular fragment by molecular fragment, potentially atom by atom. This means that soon computing will be everywhere: in the walls, in our furniture, in our clothing, and in our bodies and brains. We will be able to "print" human organs based on information provided to a machine. This means that we will ultimately be able to redesign and rebuild, molecule by molecule, our bodies and brains and the world with which we interact.

This means that everything will become information.

The amazing change that is reshaping the form of information is also redefining its substance, or—if you will allow me the term—the *soul* of information itself. These features, more than being just awesome technology, change our rules of order, our direction, and our sense of space.

Ideas are being created, shared, and updated continuously. The Web is a huge collective conversation going on at the same time, so much so that information no longer needs to be produced and searched for; rather, it seems to generate itself and finds us—even haunts us—in the form of e-newsletters, content updates, and messages.

As a consequence, everything becomes miscellaneous, and the responsibility to harness, critique, organize, and choose what information to pay attention to is left to the user. Given the abundance of information and information sources available, and in the absence of the gatekeepers

The Principle of Relevance

on whom we used to rely, information has greater volatility. Each user is left to his or her own when deciding how to use a certain piece of information and the level of importance to assign it. It is like being seated at a table around which everyone is talking at once: to whom do you listen, and whom do you trust?

4.   Origins of the Principle of Relevance

Having had, since early childhood, a keen interest in learning and personal development, I have developed a sort of addiction to research and study, which began in my teenage years. A new topic would catch my imagination and curiosity, be it marine biology, psychology, art history, or all the novels of an author I particularly enjoyed, and I would set off to the local library to research it. I remember spending countless hours skimming through catalogs, trying to locate the right thread of information before actually being able to access it. And as usually happens with complex research, the first bits of information I retrieved would only serve as triggers for further research. Learning the basic rudiments of a new topic would take months of dedicated afternoons. Today, a single string of research on Google allows me to access the same amount of information, or at least references to well-regarded publications, which I can then buy (within minutes and through the Internet, of course, whether in hardcopy or as an e-book or audiobook) in less than half an hour.

Several years ago, I had an interesting conversation with a friend, who claimed that the Internet would undermine people's commitment to learning. He claimed that surfing through the Internet was causing people to become dispersive and intellectually shallow, rather than more informed (I have seen this opinion repeated over and over again in very recent newspaper articles and publications).

I disagreed. Ten years ago I was deeply convinced, as I still am, that this would only be a consequence of an mindless use of the Internet.

To prove this point, and out of sheer curiosity, I decided to play a new game. I would pick a new topic each month, and every day, I would do fifteen minutes of research on it, usually starting from Google or Wikipedia. Any topic that lit up my imagination would do, as I used to do during my teenage years.

At the beginning of this process, I found that it was very easy to be pulled off track here and there by information that was connected in some way to the topic I was researching but did not move my research forward in any way. I learned very well the meaning and essence of the expression *surfing the Internet*: that particular addiction to following a string of information with no particular goal in mind, just browsing here and there and ultimately ending up nowhere. There was so much information on everything, so much content to read, so many e-newsletters for which to sign up, but ultimately, most of what seemed interesting at a first glance was actually rarely worth reading.

After noticing that I was actually wasting time more than learning anything, I was tempted to give up. However, I decided that I wanted to continue my quest with a specific goal in mind: I wanted to become a master of this research process and make the Internet my tool and playground. To do this, I had to be very firm from the start about the kinds of information strings into which I would allow myself to be drawn. To be successful, I needed to improve my focus and my intention. This entailed developing a clear vision of my goal, and then following my own lead. This process of setting up a clear research goal and then being completely focused on it, without letting myself wander without purpose, took some time to master, but eventually, it paid off. The amount of information I was able to retrieve was vast, and the knowledge I was able to build was more than I could ever have imagined. I called this process *seeking relevance*.

5. The Evolution

Where did this take me? Well, learning about a new topic every month was a game. It did not have an objective per se. It did, however, bring to my awareness that being able to navigate successfully through this rising ocean of easily and randomly available information requires the development of new skills, new thinking patterns, and new perception filters.

The sociological impacts of the information age are largely obvious and have been widely discussed. Wikipedia, the World Wide Web encyclopedia formed by content uploaded by users, is an amazing example of how digital information has reshaped people's approach to knowledge and information. Users organize information themselves, create it, and transfer it, all without material constraints. This kind of information system has revolutionized knowledge and its storage. For example, if an error is left in a regular book or encyclopedia, that error is bound to remain there until the next edition is printed. In online resources—Wikipedia as well as online newspapers—errors can be spotted and corrected almost instantly. Information can be updated as facts change. Information is no longer static.

Though the sociological impacts are unfolding with transparent, immediate effects, it is not yet entirely clear how this huge change is affecting our cognitive dynamics. Dealing with information and knowledge in such a different way is powerfully transformative for one's thinking processes. This idea kept stirring in my mind, and I kept thinking that this availability of information is so powerful, so changing, that it may be the trigger for a leap forward in our cognition processes—in other words, an evolution in human intelligence.

Alessandro Baricco, in his book *I Barbari* (*The Barbarians*), [2] acknowledges that the availability to everyone of technique and knowledge is creating in both the current and future generation a mutation, a transformation into a different type of human being. This feels to the so-called old generation like an invasion of barbarians—flat, soulless beings—because the availability-of-everything, but the lack of time to submerse oneself deeply into a subject, creates an apparent lack of depth.

---

[2] Alessandro Baricco, *I Barbari* (La Repubblica, 2006).

Don Tapscott and Anthony A. Williams, in their inspiring and optimistic book *Wikinomics*,[3] also explore critiques of what they call the "dark side" of the net revolution: the absence of traditional knowledge and information gatekeepers (those with the requisite knowledge to be knowledge creators and sharers) creates the potential for a slippery fall into mass mediocrity. How can one be confident that the information received is trustworthy? Mass collaboration may ensure that errors are immediately corrected, but even collaboration has pitfalls. It is well known that there is a general tendency of the masses to follow the opinions strongly expressed by a leading group of people,[4] and this may allow errors to go unnoticed or mainstream opinions to be formed without substantive background.

As a proponent of the Internet's positive force in bringing about knowledge and opportunities, I believe that with some deliberate effort, we can counterbalance this dark side and harness the enormous power of the net revolution to bring about a shift to a new generation.

I am not an anthropologist, so I will not formulate this idea in scientific terms, and I will try to state the concepts in the simplest way possible. I strongly believe that we are on the verge of a new evolution. The triggering factor of this evolution is the following: in the previous era, individual success was greatly determined by the individual's ability to

---

[3] Tapscott and Williams, *Wikinomics*.
[4] Morris Mitchell Waldrop, in *Complexity: The Emerging Science at the Edge of Order and Chaos* (Simon and Schuster, 1992), explains in simple terms the sociological and economic phenomenon by which, when an idea reaches a critical mass, it creates reinforcing thoughts and behaviors that influence people's choices, and following the law of increasing returns, it is almost impossible at that point to stop its life cycle and increasing growth.

access information. Such information was then processed in a linear way. Now everyone, or nearly everyone, has access to information; everyone is at the same level, and that differentiating factor of ability to access no longer exists. A step up has been made.

Human beings now need to learn to use information in a different way and to evolve in their cognitive abilities by moving away from linear processing. The new way means learning to scan and process different items of information at the same time, making sense of them all and choosing a response based on *relevance*. For every individual, the difference between success and failure will be shaped by his or her ability to navigate through this vast, overwhelming amount of information and stimuli available and then select, access, and use the information that is most *relevant* in the moment in reaching the individual's objective.

The information age is, essentially, the age in which those who are apt at knowledge working will gain a competitive edge. As cognitive leaps often bring about physical and genetic changes in our thought processes and neural connections, this evolution will shape the genes of the next generation of humanity.

6.   The Principle of Relevance

But how do we become skillful knowledge workers? The availability of information is itself a self-perpetuating factor that creates events, opportunities, and stimuli. How do we use the enormous wealth of information available to create a Bensalem (the utopist city described by Francis Bacon in his 1626 book *The New Atlantis*), rather than a world of confused randomness?

Knowledge working at this level requires the development, or refinement, of the following three core skills:

1.   the ability to identify one's options with crystal clarity in order to navigate through ambiguous and conflicting goals and priorities

2.   a refined situational awareness and a highly developed ability to see patterns

3.   a cultivated attention power coupled with self-knowledge and internal strength

These entail a value transformation and the development of skills such as intuiting, integrating, innovating, designing, sensing, scanning, patterning, synthesizing, judging, and knowing. To enhance one's ability to make use of the wealth of information available, one must develop the capability to see overall patterns, integrate knowledge from different sources, understand intuitively the knowledge that is essential for a given task, differentiate between trustworthy knowledge and developing knowledge, and synthesize all of this into a body of information that will

23

enable one to make decisions and reach an objective not only efficiently, but effectively.

This represents an evolutionary transformation from a traditional, linear way of processing information. The key to this transformation lies in developing a new mind-set and new tools that will enable one to harness the incredible power of information, without being overwhelmed by it, in other words, understanding and applying that special set of skills that I have come to identify as the power of *relevance.*

This involves not only learning new skills, but reeducating oneself on how to find, value, and analyze information so that knowledge working becomes an unconscious process, a new way of thinking—a new, evolutionary, cognitive way of being.

Chapter 1 – Snapshot

- Today's constant swirl of digital information exchange and retrieval often makes us feel as if we have lost control of our time.

- The radical evolution brought about by information availability and Web 2.0 information sharing facilitates the creation, consumption, and manipulation of knowledge. Wealth, time, and resources no longer constitute a barrier to knowledge and learning.

- Information is no longer something material, organized in a hierarchical way. It no longer requires expert knowledge to be produced and managed. As a consequence, everything becomes miscellaneous, and the responsibility to harness, critique, organize, and choose what information to pay attention to is left to the user.

- The sociological impacts of the information age have been widely discussed. It is not yet clear, however, how the information age is affecting our cognitive dynamics. Dealing with information and knowledge in such a different way is transformative for our thinking processes.

- As information becomes accessible, we move away from linear processing and learn to scan and process different items of information at the same time, making sense of them all and choosing a response based on relevance. This involves a cognitive leap.

- The difference between success and failure is no longer based on availability of information, but rather on the ability to navigate through an overwhelming amount of data and select, access, and use the information that is most *relevant*.

- Artful knowledge workers have a competitive edge in the information age. As cognitive leaps often bring about physical and genetic changes in thought processes and neural connections, this evolution will shape the genes of the next generation of humanity.

- Knowledge working at this level requires three core skills: (1) the ability to identify one's options; (2) a refined situational awareness and a highly developed ability to see patterns; and (3) a cultivated attention power together with self-knowledge and internal strength.

- By reeducating oneself on how to find, value, and analyze information, knowledge working becomes an unconscious process, a new way of thinking—a new cognitive way of being.

The Principle of Relevance

TWO

Relevance: The Fundamentals

1. The Definitions

Relevance is a term normally used to describe how pertinent, connected, or applicable something (information, an event, a document, but also thought, action, and behavior) is to a given matter. A thing is relevant if it serves as a means to a specified purpose. In the context of information retrieval, relevance defines how well a specific material or element of data meets the topic of the query.

A number of philologists in the last two decades have drawn attention to the importance of relevance decisions in both reasoning and communication. They note that any information is delivered within a context, and its relevance depends on the state of knowledge of the subject who encounters that information.[5]

This theory, though it seems to apply well to the relationships between communication and interpretation of information exchanged between individuals, encounters difficulties when it is applied to problems that do not involve a direct interaction between two persons. Other authors have addressed this gap by attempting to define relevance as goal-dependent: an

---

[5] See, in particular, Dan Sperber and Deirdre Wilson, *Relevance: Communication and Cognition* (Blackwell, 1986/1985).

item (e.g., a piece of information or an object) is relevant to a goal if and only if it can be an essential element of some plan capable of achieving the desired goal.[6]

Trying to find an objective parameter for evaluating relevance is, however, problematic. For example, a piece of information may be more or less relevant, depending on the order and timing in which all pieces of information are received. Relevance therefore seems to be a rather subjective parameter, essentially denoting a *relationship* between an item and another item that is taken as a parameter (what the *relevant thing* is *relevant to*).

2. Consciousness and the Ability of the Mind to Process Information

However you may prefer to define relevance, you are, at this point, certainly aware that at any given time, your brain is being bombarded with millions of bits of information, and it needs to filter through this information to find what is relevant for it, according to the relevance parameters it has set.

The function of conscious awareness, the result of complex biological processes, is to represent information about what is happening outside and inside the organism in such a way that it can be evaluated and acted on by the body. A person perceives through a complex series of active perpetual

---

[6] See B. Gorayska and R. O. Lindsay in a series of articles published in *Journal of Pragmatics* 19 (1993).

The Principle of Relevance

filters. The world as perceived is a map created by our neurology: a person's body transmits certain information to the brain through the senses, and the brain processes it according to certain categories it has created throughout the person's life, based on the person's education, cultural background, and experiences. What one pays attention to in the map is further filtered through personal beliefs, interests, and preoccupations. In this sense, it functions as a clearinghouse for sensations, perceptions, feelings, and ideas, establishing priorities among all the diverse pieces of information ingested into the brain. Without consciousness, one would still know what is going on but would have to react to it in a reflexive, instinctive way. With consciousness, one can deliberately weigh the information that the senses produce and respond accordingly.

The nervous system has a definite limit to how much information it can process at any given time. Only a limited number of inputs can simultaneously appear in consciousness and be recognized and handled appropriately before they begin to crowd each other out. For example, while logically thinking about a problem, you cannot truly experience a strong emotion, sing, and make calculations simultaneously because each of these activities exhausts most of your capacity for attention.

According to scientific research proposed by American psychologist George Miller in his research article "The Magic Number Seven, Plus or

Minus Two,"[7] concerning the capacity of people to store and transmit information, the conscious brain can only process a maximum of seven bits of information at any given time (e.g., differentiated sounds, visual stimuli, or recognizable nuances of emotion and thought); the shortest time it takes to discriminate between one set of bits and another is about 1/18 of a second. This seems, at first glance, like a huge amount, but it really is not, considering that this includes everything the brain must process at any given moment—every external input, thought, memory, feeling, and action.

This study has been the subject of many reviews and critiques throughout the years. Mainly, the number 7 is not obviously a definite measurement: there is no objective evidence to support this specific number, which derives mainly from experiential exploration. It is generally accepted now that the actual measurement of what the human brain can process can vary greatly, depending on the combination between perceptual and mnemonic processes: our innate or acquired ability to subdivide and organize information into smaller chunks, the variety of stimuli available, a particular familiarity with the language being used or the task being performed, and training. However, this does not alter the substantial and experimentally verifiable issue that the short-term memory,

---

[7] George A. Miller, "The Magic Number Seven, Plus or Minus Two: Some Limits on Our Capacity for Processing Information," *The Psychological Review* 101 (1956): 343–352.

The Principle of Relevance

one's immediate conscious awareness, has limited storage and processing capacity.

Over time, humans have learned to chunk bits of information into smaller pieces and delegate more menial tasks so that certain processes become automated. The ability to compress stimuli allows us to intake and process larger chunks of data. By compounding information, you can extend this capacity and your span of attention.

For example, learning how to drive a car with the goal of reaching a destination, when taken from a point outside the process, involves taking in many points of information at once: the position of your foot on the gas pedal; when and how to move your foot to the brake pedal; locating, reading, understanding, and then reacting appropriately to street signs and traffic lights; seeing, understanding, and evaluating the intent of other drivers; and then from this, anticipating their next moves and how these moves relate to your own moves. However, with practice, these parts, which, prior to experience, comprised driving as a whole, can be broken down in the mind into separate, smaller, identifiable actions, and certain of these, such as moving your feet on the pedals and responding to traffic lights, become relegated to unconscious parts of the mind and thus become unconscious tasks, making the overall goal of driving the car—to reach a certain destination—the only conscious activity on which your mind needs to focus.

Once the basics of operating the car become unconscious, room is left in the mind to process not only the end goal—reaching your destination—

but also other activities such as thinking about what to make for dinner, how to best approach that new client, or whether to stop for a snack. In this way, the mind has learned to compress one very complicated task that would otherwise take up all your cognitive resources, so that now, driving can occur simultaneously with another task.

However, although you may continuously learn and acquire techniques to process more data at once, you can only respond to limited data. This means, for example, that theoretically, you could process simultaneously a person talking to you (mainly auditory information) and an e-mail (mainly visual information), but to do so, you must keep out of consciousness every other thought or sensation. This means that you couldn't be aware of the speaker's expressions, and wonder why he is saying what he is saying, and notice what he is wearing, and ask a question.

3. The Essentials of Time Management

Time management skills, or the lack thereof, is a consumed topic explored by a plethora of books and educational programs.

As you say yes or no to things that are presented to you during your day, you may often feel that time is consumed by things that really don't matter to you and that there is never enough time for the things you really want or need to do. This perceived difficulty, however, is often due not so much to an actual lack of time or inability to manage time, but rather to a more fundamental issue: the inability to prioritize and organize one's schedule on the basis of specific priorities.

An essential point raised by Stephen R. Covey in his classic book *The 7 Habits of Highly Effective People*[8] is that you may be very well versed in managing and organizing time, and have taken sophisticated time management courses, but still feel you are not using time wisely. This is essentially because the ability to manage time well doesn't make any difference if you are organizing your time around activities that are not priorities for you.

In his book, Covey describes the various types of situations we encounter on a daily basis and how most people usually manage them by dividing situations into four categories:

1. *Important and urgent.* Real critical situations that require immediate and focused attention.

2. *Important and not urgent.* Mid-term and long-term goals, and those elements that make your life enjoyable and happy, that are important to you.

3. *Not important and urgent.* Matters that are screaming for your immediate attention but would essentially be avoidable if important and not urgent items are consistently prioritized.

4. *Not important and not urgent.* This is self-explanatory.

---

[8] Stephen R. Covey, *The 7 Habits of Highly Effective People* (Fireside, 1990).

The Principle of Relevance

The essence of this categorization is that urgent is very different from important. An urgent matter is simply something that demands your attention; its essential quality is that it calls you to action immediately. Something urgent, however, may or may not be important. Most people's lives are consumed by N. 1 (important and urgent) and N. 3 (not important and urgent) situations: important and urgent situations usually compose a much longer list than they should because when you are in an overwhelmed state, you don't deal with important activities until they become urgent. You may also be consumed by N. 3 (not important and urgent) activities because you tend to respond to what is urgent—and important to others but not necessarily important to you—simply because it is screaming for your attention and you are compelled to get it out of your way.

The key to effective time management, according to this classic, and always valid, principle, is dealing with important matters that support or relate to your life purpose, vision, or preferred lifestyle before they become urgent. This requires a clear sense of priority and a high degree of effort and self-mastery. The reward is that by consistently giving priority to that which is important, you are able to deal with most situations before they become urgent; your list of the important and urgent becomes thinner and ultimately includes only real emergencies.

4.   Time Management in a Data Overload Era

The basics of time management, as discussed in the preceding section, are core essentials in every person's daily life. However, they assume linear, item-by-item processing.

This system may sometimes feel simplistic and overloaded in an era when the quantity of external (data, requests, and events) and internal (thoughts and reactions) stimuli we deal with on a daily basis increases continuously so that priorities constantly shift. In this scenario, it is very difficult to decide what is important, and everything seems urgent.

Those of you who work in a corporate environment are well aware of how the number of e-mails received on any ordinary day seems to increase at constant speed. In addition, social interactions are becoming less predictable and more difficult to manage. Information, rather than being something we look for, is starting to find us, looks for us, and sometimes even haunts us. Think about the e-newsletters, social networking sites, daily news digests, and e-mails pushed constantly on your mobile device all day long.

There are so many data that need to be processed, and processed fast, that it is easy to feel constantly overwhelmed and unable to control the direction of your life. Every day becomes exhausting; all we feel is an increasing demand for production and efficiency.

This applies to all areas of life: work and social interactions are both affected. The overflow of data and stimuli also produces more mental

34

activity, more thoughts, which in turn produce more data and stimuli in a self-feeding growth system. As a consequence, even an individual's priorities—those elements that would go into the important and urgent category—seem to shift constantly.

While production may seem to increase, efficiency, however, never does, as more production seems to produce an ever increasing flow of demands, which may overload a person with data, requests, events, and thoughts—in other words, things that call for immediate attention.

This causes great anxiety in most people as one does not know to which tasks one should devote energy and time. As the daily information overload drama unfolds, several questions become increasingly essential: what is worth knowing? What is worth doing? What is worth responding to?

5.   Intent or Content: The Hidden Paradox of Communication

This is also very obvious in the context of social interactions via electronic means.

Whenever you are engaged in a conversation, you have in your mind your own notion of what content you think is relevant to communicate to the other person. The other person has his or her own notion of relevance in mind, which may be very different from yours.

Whatever each person verbalizes in the interaction, it is because he or she believes that the message is relevant enough to be worth communicating. In a social or professional interaction, you normally respond to the input sent out by the other person, therefore keeping the conversation going, because you instinctively feel that if the other person is sending you a certain message, it is relevant enough to be worth processing.

This automatic response instinct is obviously essential in personal interactions that involve one-on-one conversations and, in general, for building social relationships. The "if a message is verbalized, it's worth processing" instinct, however, no longer proves true in our complex world of multileveled digital interactions, in which a number of different messages are sent through to us at the same time by different people. The digital world requires an assessment of whether the message is worth processing.

This can be done by acknowledging that a communication itself will implicitly make manifest nothing else but the intent to communicate. This does not mean that the actual content of the communication is relevant, per se, for the mere fact that it was communicated to you.

6. The Principle of Relevance

One's immediate reaction to an overload of inputs is to try to tackle every input in accordance with a principle of efficiency—getting more things done—which often translates into responding to everything. Efficiency, in its original sense, means using resources to maximize productivity, measured as a ratio of output (production) to input (the resources needed for production: time, energy, money, work). Enhancing productivity and efficiency is useless per se if it does not serve the purpose of reaching your ultimate goals, whatever they might be.

It is possible to be really busy, even extremely efficient and productive, without actually being effective, without actually achieving your objectives. Working uniquely on the basis of an efficiency principle, as most people tend to do, means you get sidetracked into responding to and processing all inputs as they come, using the resources and information available to you to process and respond as completely as possible, and in the shortest amount of time. This, however, does not necessarily help you stay on purpose.

Effectiveness is substantially different from efficiency and may be defined as the power to produce a desired effect, in other words, the ability to do the right thing at the right time to reach a definite goal. Effectiveness per se is not a function of the resources spent in achieving that goal. While effectiveness is also normally efficient (although in some cases, it may not be), efficiency may or may not be effective.

Effectiveness is not about using maximum energy all the time; rather, it is about calibrating energy and focus. Effectiveness does not mean processing all messages, but rather, learning how to identify those messages that are relevant to your purpose and respond only to them. You may recall the example described in chapter 1: it is easy to become sidetracked from reaching a determined objective when in the middle of an information overflow—in an attempt to be efficient, you feel compelled to respond to every e-mail as it comes and to take care of every last-

The Principle of Relevance

minute emergency, thus getting off-task, until the working day is over and you have not accomplished anything of real substance.

Human beings naturally react to situations that are put in front of them. As we have seen, whenever an input reaches your brain, you are used to reacting to it based on the underlying unconscious assumption that any information addressed to you is worth processing. As such, you may often be sidetracked into responding to and acting on the assumption that all information addressed to you conveys the presumption of its own relevance.

The current information age has moved us from a place of obvious relevance—when you are being addressed by one person in a face-to-face conversation—to a new situation, similar to being in a room where five, ten, even one hundred people are facing you and talking to you at once. Your immediate instinct is to try to respond to each one in turn, to treat each conversation in a one-on-one, face-to-face manner, or alternatively, to shut everyone out and not respond to anything. To adapt your response and communication instincts to the information age, you need to learn how to filter out quickly the many faces in the crowd and focus on the one face addressing you with the inputs you need or to which you want to dedicate attention—those inputs that are *relevant* for you.

There is therefore one principle which, applied consistently, trains you to override the challenges of the information age and take advantage of the wave of opportunities it presents, without being crushed by it. As the

The Principle of Relevance

human brain works more easily with definitions, we will call this the *principle of relevance.*

Acting on the basis of the *principle of relevance* means expanding your brain's capability to acquire and process data, while at the same time having the ability and mastery to discriminate the data which are relevant and respond to those, and those only. In other words, the *principle of relevance* is based on two concepts:

1. ***Creative intake*:** letting inputs come in

2. ***Deliberate action*:** responding only to those inputs to which you choose to respond

At any given time, to be able to reach an objective effectively, you need to be able to recognize what is *relevant* for you in relation to that objective and what is not, and then take deliberate action by responding to that which is *relevant* only. Most readers will think that they are already perfectly capable of doing so. Indeed, each person has this innate capability, but do you really apply it in practice? Take an honest look at your life, your ordinary day. You will notice that you apply this skill less and less and spend most of your time reacting to inputs as they come, rather than sorting them out in accordance with your *relevance* principle. More often than not, this does not get you what you want, or if it does, it is at a very high price in terms of effort, time, and sacrifice. Being able to recognize *relevance* is mainly an intellectual exercise, but actually applying it involves a further step: not only intelligence and understanding, but also attention, control, and self-mastery.

Learning to recognize and act on the *principle of relevance* empowers you to become a skillful knowledge worker by bridging the gap between responses and intentions: what you do, and what you are actually trying to achieve by doing it.

Filtering your actions through the *principle of relevance* improves your discernment abilities, helps you perceive clearly through your mind or senses, and aids in processing information quickly. The objective being to retrieve only the information that is useful to you and act only on that information, letting go all else that calls your attention but is not useful for you.

Ancient master Sun Tzu, in the book *The Art of War*,[9] clearly spells out the principle that ultimate excellence lies not in fighting every battle, but in knowing when to get into the arena and when to pull out. This will not only make you more effective, but it will also result in greater enjoyment of each activity. Psychologists have demonstrated that a person who is able to enjoy the activities he or she pursues is one who has chosen whatever choice he or she is pursuing.

But how do you develop that "knowing" ability? How do you refine your ability to recognize relevance?

---

[9] Sun Tzu, *The Art of War*, sixth century B.C. (various editions and translations available).

Chapter 2 – Snapshot

- Relevance is a term normally used to describe how pertinent, connected, or applicable something is to a given matter. Trying to find an objective parameter for evaluating relevance is, however, problematic: relevance is a subjective parameter essentially denoting a relationship (what the *relevant thing* is *relevant to*).

- The brain is bombarded with millions of bits of data, which it needs to filter through in order to find what is useful: most of that information is not relevant. While we have acquired techniques that enable our brains to process multiple data at once, we can only respond to limited data at any given time.

- Time management skills have been widely covered in literature. The skills we have been taught are essential but assume a linear, item-by-item method of processing. This system may sometimes seem simplistic and overloaded when the quantity of external and internal stimuli with which each one of us needs to deal increases daily in all areas of life. The overflow of data and stimuli also produces more mental activity, more thoughts, which in turn produce more data and stimuli in a self-feeding growth system. As a consequence, even priorities shift constantly.

- As our daily information overload drama unfolds, several questions become more and more essential: what is worth knowing? What is worth doing? What is worth responding to?

- In personal interactions, you respond to inputs sent out by the other person because you feel that if the other person is sending you a message, it is relevant enough to be worth processing. This automatic response instinct is essential in interactions that involve a one-on-one conversation, but it does not apply in the world of multileveled digital interactions, where a number of different messages are sent through to us at the same time by different people. The digital world requires an assessment as to whether the message is worth processing. A communication itself will implicitly make manifest *the intent to communicate*: this does not mean that the actual content of the communication is relevant per se for the mere fact of being

The Principle of Relevance

communicated.

- One's immediate reaction to an overload of inputs is to try to tackle every input in accordance with a principle of efficiency—getting more things done—which often translates into responding to everything.

- Effectiveness, on the other hand, is the power to produce a desired effect: the ability to do the right thing at the right time to reach a definite goal. While effectiveness is also normally efficient, efficiency may or may not be effective.

- The information age creates a situation similar to being in a room where one hundred people are talking to you at once. Your immediate instinct is to try to respond to each one in turn, to treat each conversation in a one-on-one manner, or alternatively, to shut everyone out and not respond to anything. To adapt your response and communication instincts to the information age, you need to learn how to filter out quickly those different inputs, to focus in on the one face addressing you with the information you need or to which you want to dedicate attention—that which is are relevant for you.

- Acting on the basis of the principle of relevance means expanding your brain's capability to acquire and process multilayered and fast flowing data, while at the same time having the ability and mastery to sort out, among those data, which are relevant and respond to those, and those only.

- The principle of relevance is based on two concepts: (1) creative intake, or letting inputs come in, and (2) deliberate action, or responding only to those inputs to which you choose to respond.

The Principle of Relevance

THREE

Finding Relevance: Navigating Complexity

1.   The Mastery of Complexity

The complexity of our time requires the processing of ever expanding amounts of data day to day, hour to hour, and moment to moment. There is no time to give things focus and considered thought. Or at least, that is the excuse the mind often produces. In reality, it is possible; you simply have to train yourself to do it.

When the brain is faced with a problem, it rapidly collects what data it can. As the information begins to come in, the brain rapidly accepts the information and fits it into some preexisting category, discarding what seems irrelevant. When enough information is processed to provide a conclusion, it takes action on the conclusion, deletes the information that wasn't apparently supportive, and files only the material that supported its decisions. Then, it moves on to the next processing requirement.

You may have observed that as you are inundated with more and more data, the amount of information you allow your brain to collect and process begins to decrease, and you have a tendency to reach quick conclusions. This is because, in an attempt to defend yourself from an overwhelming overload of data, your brain may respond by cutting down data gathering and responding immediately and more quickly than necessary to everything in an unconscious attempt to limit that overload. As a consequence, your actions and responses risk being desultory, random, and removed from context.

You may have found yourself in a situation in which you come back from an overseas trip and you find yourself overwhelmed with e-mails. In an attempt to get through the daunting hundreds of e-mails and back to work, you respond to each one in turn, without first scrolling through the subject lines and senders. You may soon realize that you responded to one client without having read later messages from the same client and end up embarrassed to have to send another e-mail (or two, or three) to the same recipient, backtracking on your first response and looking very unprofessional.

The principle of relevance consists of expanding the amount of information you are able to let in, while at the same time being able to invest the right amount of energy in the right place at the right time in your response to that information input, eliminating the unnecessary, responding only to what is relevant, and seeing the big picture with a strong awareness of priorities—the reverse of what most people do.

So how do you achieve this? To master the principle of relevance, you have to work with the following elements:

The Principle of Relevance

1.   **clarity of purpose**

2.   **situational awareness**

3.   **pattern discernment**

4.   **attention**

5.   **self-knowledge and self-mastery**

In this chapter, I will discuss the main concepts underlying these points. In part II, I will give you some practical tools to exercise your mind using these points. While these five concepts can be teased apart, functionally and cognitively, they work together and blend together as integral, overlapping parts of the principle of relevance. They are therefore to be viewed as parts of an integrated system, constantly overlapping and dynamically interacting with each other.

2.   Relevance Principle N. 1 - Clarity of Purpose

Step 1—What Are the Options?

Goal-setting seminars and self-help books are widely spread in the market, and everyone has been lectured at least once on the importance of setting clear goals. It is indeed impossible to be effective without a clear outcome in mind. Most people think that the reason why they don't get things done or don't achieve their objectives is a lack of discipline or the quantity or complexity of their work. Taking a closer look, you will see this is not usually the case.

45

The problem, more often than not, is not the work, nor the complexity of it. Usually, objectives are not being met because of an inability to set a clear purpose for action, to set priorities, and to develop the self-mastery to maintain purpose and priorities with attention and focus.

This becomes increasingly difficult when you experience inner conflict. Inner conflict is the result of competing claims on your energy and attention. To reduce this conflict and make a decision, it is essential to sort out the possibilities, become aware of what the options and conflicting alternatives are, and arbitrate between them by making a conscious choice.

No matter how sophisticated your intelligence or how strong your mind, willpower alone cannot pull you through the continuous stream of external inputs and requests unless you have formed a clear idea of what you want to achieve. Once you have made the effort to recognize that priority, opportunities and information will automatically follow, and effectiveness with them.

You have to be very clear about the result you want to achieve. This can be a small step of a longer-term result, and you may change it over time if you feel that it does not suit you; however, to take any meaningful step, you must choose a direction. The more precisely and positively you can define what you want, the more you program your brain to seek out and notice possibilities. Therefore the more likely you are to stay on purpose. It is a commonsense observation that opportunities exist when they are recognized as such, and yet it is very easy for the mind to glaze over potential opportunities simply because, not having set a purpose

The Principle of Relevance

clearly, it cannot process the event or information as related to that purpose.

Setting a purpose requires not only clear thinking, in which you are probably well trained; also, first and foremost, it requires a clear awareness of all the available options. In haste to make decisions, most people often tend to overlook this essential step.

For example, when you are embarking on a work project, you may think that the goal is clear and doesn't require much exploration. If you take a closer look, however, you will realize that your ultimate purpose is not so immediate and that you could have a number of hidden goals in your subconscious mind that you have not considered. For example, some possible options from which to choose your primary purpose are suggested in Table 3.1

Table 3.1. Primary purpose options

Option 1	To deliver a perfectly thought-through project according to your highest standards
Option 2	To contribute a meaningful and innovative idea
Option 3	To impress your boss to get closer to a promotion or obtain more responsibility
Option 4	To win the trust of a new client
Option 5	To get the work done as quickly as possible and move on to some other activity

The Principle of Relevance

Before starting to work on the project, you will need to clarify to yourself, as honestly as possible, what your real goal is. If you achieve this clarity, the actions required to achieve your outcome will easily follow.

The style of your work and the things to which you need to pay attention could be very different, depending on the real purpose for your actions. Your supervisor, for example, might have very specific requirements and preferences that are not necessarily congruent with the ones you would choose if your goal were to deliver a perfectly thought-through project according to your own standards. Contributing a meaningful and innovative idea might require you to rethink your usual parameters and work with a different perspective, taking risks you wouldn't otherwise consider. If your goal is to get a new client, you will need to tailor your project to a specific quality that will break through for that client, for example, speed and ease of reading. If your goal is to get the work done as quickly as possible, you might want to skip over certain bits that could be intellectually enjoyable if your goal were to deliver a perfectly thought-through project according to your highest standards, but that you don't have the interest or the time to do.

As you can see, becoming aware of your true purpose is a delicate and fundamental process needed before embarking on any new project. Once you have clearly defined a purpose, you will evaluate the relevance of inputs, resources, and information based on that specific purpose and become deliberate in your actions and responses.

The Principle of Relevance

Step 2—The Evidence Procedure

Have you ever realized that you tend to pay attention only to those things that are important to you at a given time? If your dominant thoughts are about creating a new business, you'll start paying attention to interesting business ventures on the market.

If your dominant thoughts are about someone to whom you are romantically attracted, you will notice every bit of information that relates to her or reminds you of her. This principle is so simple and works at such a deep level that we are often not even aware it is occurring. Bringing it to a conscious level creates a very powerful shift of awareness and is an example of the process your brain uses as it chooses what it will pay attention to.

Several studies have tried to explain how this process works in the brain, and recently, a number of modern authors and neuroscientists have offered the theory that our brain includes a particular system that acts as a sort of "control center." This "control center" acts by filtering the sensory input that the brain draws from the external world and sorts out the torrent of incoming information, sending a signal to the appropriate part of the brain for processing the information that it deems relevant for your brain. It then chooses what to accept and reject based on what you have chosen to pay attention to, plus your beliefs, values, and prejudices.

A very important but often overlooked step after determining your purpose is to decide on your evidence procedure. How will you know if your outcome meets your values? The difficulty lies in the fact that the goals of an activity are not always clear and the feedback is often ambiguous. If you are baking a cake, you need to know how sweet you want it, how soft, how much vanilla flavor you want to taste, and so on. If you had no evidence procedure, you would go round and round the loop forever because you would never know when to stop. You have to know when you have reached your objective.

In this process, you also have to keep your senses open so that you notice what feedback you are getting and if you are going in the right direction. You must train yourself in sensory acuity: where to place your attention and for how long. This may also mean heightened awareness of your internal images, sounds, and feelings. You need to develop the sensory acuity, or sensitivity, to notice if what you are paying attention to is relevant. Exercises to train yourself to do this are included in the next chapters.

As we have seen previously, our conscious awareness can only process a limited amount of bits of information at any given time. Consider the million bits of information with which your brain is assaulted every second: everything you see, hear, smell, feel, and touch is a message entering your brain. It is obvious that your nervous system goes through a process of deletion, distortion, and generalization in order for you to make sense of all the data it is required to digest.

While I leave you to further reading to understand more about these processes and the related neuroscientific experiments (see the bibliography), the essential and experimental value to be learned from this

The Principle of Relevance

is that your mind-set reflects your sense of purpose, and your sense of purpose organizes your perceptions. It is therefore essential to become conscious about setting a very specific purpose and evidence procedure. Explore all your options, set your objective, and decide on an evidence procedure; otherwise, you will overlook the information, resources, connections, and events that will assist you in effectively reaching your objective.

3. Relevance Principle N. 2—Situational Awareness

The second main skill you need to build is the ability to become aware of the environment, situation, and resources with which you are dealing in an objective and realistic manner. Part of this awareness is understanding the situation in context: the current dynamics of your environment, the multiple forces involved in the complexity of relationships, the many aspects of events that are governed by human emotion. The increase in the quantity and speed of data and information flow makes situational awareness a challenging but essential skill.

Situational awareness may be defined as the ability to create, acknowledge, and understand a comprehensive and coherent situational representation of an existing situation that is not static, but rather, continuously updated in accordance with the results of recurrent situation assessments. It involves the ability to combine new information with existing knowledge stored in memory and the development of a composite picture of the situation along with projections of future status and subsequent decisions as to appropriate courses of action to take. In terms

The Principle of Relevance

of what it requires for the mind, it is the ability to maintain a constant, clear mental picture of relevant information and its interactions with a complex, dynamic environment.

In the business project situation discussed in chapter 1 with Chris and his or her boss, a highly developed situational awareness would allow Chris's boss to realize that the effect of asking Chris to deal immediately with an issue presented as urgent is to delay the broader analysis that would actually provide an answer to this issue as well as giving a partial response that will probably need to be changed later as it will not take the bigger picture into account.

In situations of high data flow, situational awareness is extremely important. The importance and impact of situational awareness have been the increased object of scientific studies in recent years, mostly in relation to critical environments in which a lack of awareness or missing information can make the difference between life and death such as the military, aviation, and medical fields. In relation to the military, for example, situational awareness will impact the ability to understand a specific situation that enables a commander to place current battlefield events into context; to readily share a portrayal of the situation with staff and subordinates; and to predict, expect, and prepare for future states and actions of the enemy.

Though most readers would not often find themselves making similar life-and-death decisions, situational awareness and its importance can readily move from the battlefield to everyday life. The earlier narrative about the complexities of driving a car is clearly reflective of ongoing situational analysis. Likewise, stockbrokers practice situational analysis to advise clients and play the market effectively, just as an effective business owner needs to take into account his competitors' foreseeable moves and the general market trends when making a business plan for the year ahead.

The most common theoretical framework of situational awareness is provided, among others, in a number of related publications by Dr. Mica Endsley.[10] According to Endsley, three stages, or steps, of situational awareness formation can be elucidated: perception, comprehension, and projection.

Level 1—Perception

The first step in achieving situational awareness is to perceive the status, attributes, and dynamics of relevant elements in an environment. Perception involves monitoring, observing, and recognizing what is going on. It leads to an awareness of multiple situational elements (objects, events, people, systems, environmental factors) and their current states (spatial components, conditions, modes, actions). Perception is knowledge.

---

[10] *Designing for Situation Awareness: An Approach to Human-Centered Design*, M. R. Endsley, B. Bolte, and D. G. Jones (Taylor & Francis, 2003), and *Situation Awareness Analysis and Measurement*, M. R. Endsley and D. J. Garland (eds.) (Lawrence Erlbaum, 2000).

The Principle of Relevance

Level 2—Comprehension

Comprehension involves integrating data as perceived in their context and making sense of them. At this level, the disjointed intake of information perceived in level 1 is synthesized through the processes of pattern recognition, interpretation, and evaluation. The information is interpreted and integrated in a comprehensive, contextual way. Comprehension answers the question "so what?" Comprehension is knowledge and understanding.

Level 3—Projection

The third level of situational awareness involves the ability to project the future actions of the elements in the environment, building on the knowledge processed through levels 1 and 2. Once the status and dynamics of a situation are known (level 1) and comprehended (level 2), the information then needs to be projected forward in time to determine how it will affect the evolution of a certain situation. Projection is increasingly difficult in situations in which new data and inputs continuously enter the system, as this requires a continuous updating of the mental representation deriving from perception and comprehension and reassessment of the results of projection.

4.   Relevance Principle N. 3—The Ability to Perceive Patterns

As we have seen, a fundamental aspect of the comprehension level in situational awareness is the ability to see and perceive patterns. Pattern recognition is such a fundamental and distinctive skill that it is worthy of separate discussion.

The ability to detect patterns out of oceans of disparate data requires perception of the underlying regularities in data and information. This has become a central skill for today's world. This ability, essentially based on inductive logic, involves accepting and perceiving the flow of raw data in all its volume and chaotic naturalness, rather than focusing on single data elements and then inferring from seemingly disconnected data the patterns that lie underneath. This skill is the essence of the scientific method, but unfortunately, much of our educational system and work environments often train the brain to do just the opposite. In Western school systems, we are rarely trained to find information and make sense of it in the overall context by making connections and identifying relationships. Instead, we are often trained to process, analyze, and memorize information per se, as if a piece of information (an algebraic equation, a rule of grammar, an historical event) had some essential value in itself, regardless of context. Students are pressured to remember, rather than understand, the information they intake. However, when the brain is pressured to remember each single item of data it encounters, each item assumes an importance that it normally does not have in the overall system, so that each single bit of information seems to be apt at producing major changes

55

in the whole underlying system. This entails that eventually, one will conclude that developing different intellectual skills altogether and a focused and singular dedication are required, for example, to master algebra, music, or a foreign language. Most people bring this same distortion to their working lives, tackling each problem as if it were essential, unique, and disconnected from the general flow of things. When working on this basis, an individual often finds that he or she is able to make quick decisions when confronted with a problem that has identical characteristics to an issue already encountered in the past, but the individual may find himself or herself struggling with situations that seem unique. The ability to be aware of patterns, on the other hand, allows the individual to see how the components of solutions generated in one area can apply to other areas.

The ability to see and perceive patterns takes time and effort to develop; however, once developed, it unfolds the skill of quickly perceiving and understanding large quantities of data and making quick decisions based on those data. These connections do not typically arrive through direct conscious effort, as when working on a logical analogy in which relationships can be intentionally paired.

Perceiving patterns requires the ability to shift context fluidly and make new connections in a way that allows harmonious, fluid movement between the left and right hemispheres of the brain.

You can imagine it as the ability to see the forest and the trees: to zoom out to assess macro patterns of the forest, while also zooming in and

The Principle of Relevance

identifying the single tree. For this reason, when you train your pattern recognition abilities to be highly sophisticated, more often than not, you will recognize patterns subconsciously and at great speed.

Exercise and time dedicated to developing pattern recognition abilities make it possible, over time, to make instant decisions that seem instinctual for their speed.

5.   Relevance Principle N. 4—The Attention Factor

While walking on a busy downtown road, you pass hundreds of people and cars. You might be absorbed in thought, or humming a tune, or concerned with checking that you are taking the right route if you are not familiar with the area. You may notice at one point a person who is behaving abnormally—perhaps he is walking too fast or too slow or unsteadily; perhaps he has an unusual appearance or strange clothes; perhaps something in his behavior looks aggressive; or perhaps he is unusually handsome or is wearing a perfume that immediately reminds you of someone in your past.

The realization of the unusual person enters the focus of your consciousness and you become aware of him. The mind tries to relate the visual information about that person to information about other past experiences stored in your memory, to determine into which category the present individual fits. In the context of the aggressive behavior, is he drunk? Is he angry? Is he mentally ill? Is he momentarily distracted? As soon as the event is matched to an already known class of events, it is identified. Now it must be evaluated: is this person's behavior something to worry about? If the answer is yes, then you must decide on an appropriate course of action.

All these complex mental operations are often completed in a few seconds, sometimes in a fraction of a second. The process that makes awareness rise and focus is called *attention*. It is attention that selects the relevant bits of information from the potential millions of bits available. It takes attention to retrieve the appropriate references from memory, to evaluate the event, and then to choose the right thing to do.

Despite, or as a consequence of, its power, attention can only focus on a limited amount of data. It cannot notice or hold in focus more information than that which can be processed simultaneously. Retrieving information from memory storage and bringing it into the focus of awareness, comparing information, evaluating, and deciding all make demands on the mind's limited processing capacity.

Attention is an amazing resource of our consciousness. Some people learn to use it effectively, while others waste it. The mark of a person who is effective is an ability to focus attention at will, to be oblivious to distractions, to concentrate for as long as it takes to achieve a goal, and not a minute longer, and then move on to something else.

Each person has the choice of how to use his or her attention: you can focus it intentionally and deliberately, or you can diffuse it (and waste it) in scattered, random waves.

The Principle of Relevance

The shape and content of your life depends on how you use your attention: entirely different realities emerge, depending on how attention is invested. Attention determines what will or will not appear in your consciousness, and you create your world depending on how you invest this precious resource. Memories, thoughts, and feelings are all shaped by how you use it. Attention is the mind's most powerful tool.

The psychic entropy peculiar to the human condition involves seeing more to do than one can actually accomplish and yet feeling able to accomplish more than what conditions allow: this results in the person always being driven by a natural tendency to disperse attention until the moment at which attention is forcefully driven by external demands or an emotionally charged situation. Unless a person knows how to give order to his or her thoughts, attention will be attracted to what is most problematic at the moment: thoughts or memories linked to strong emotions, external sources of information, inputs and requests. Unless directed, the normal state of the human mind seems to be chaos and entropy.

We don't usually notice how little control we have over our attention. We live based on a set of habits and social roles prescribed by culture, which channel our energy so well that our thoughts, and often even our actions, go about their own daily routine without requiring any effort on our side.

Without training, and without an object in the external world that demands attention, people are unable to focus their thoughts for more than a few minutes at a time. This leads to a sense of self-condemnation to notice and process irrelevant stimuli, to attend to everything at once and, as a result, not attend to anything at all.

Paying attention involves your time, energy, and mindfulness. It is not easy and requires deliberate effort. But when you own and connect to your attention factor, you are able to live your life in the present, and this empowers you, centers you, energizes you, keeps you in harmony and on purpose. It keeps your actions *relevant*.

6. Relevance Principle N. 5 —Self-Knowledge and Self-Mastery

The value of refined situational awareness, pattern recognition skills, and developed attention is magnified if these skills are linked to knowledge of the way one reacts to a situation. The first step in successfully applying the tools described is a thorough and deep understanding of oneself, that is, one's goals, objectives, values, limitations, internal defenses, and weaknesses of thought and action.

By knowing yourself, you learn to work within your limitations and support your strengths, thus ensuring that the data, information, and knowledge coming to you are properly identified and interpreted. For example, you may have noticed how some people obtain their best results when they work on disarming differences, while others are particularly skilled at discerning resemblances.

Self-knowledge is an old concept, which, in modern times, is also often referred to as *intrapersonal intelligence*. Intrapersonal intelligence involves knowledge of the internal aspects of the self such as awareness, knowledge and understanding of one's feelings, the range of one's own emotional responses, one's thinking processes and patterns, and one's internal inconsistencies. Intrapersonal intelligence allows a person to be conscious of his or her consciousness, that is, to step back from his or her thought patterns and watch them as an outside observer. It involves a capacity to construct an accurate perception of oneself and to use such knowledge in planning and directing one's life, to experience wholeness and unity and to discern patterns of connection within the larger order of things.

No matter how solid and consistent one thinks one may be, even in a person's own soul and personality, there are often different conflicting parts, which embody different values, are ruled by different interests, and have different intentions: they therefore conflict. This often causes incongruity in internal intentions and thought processes as mind and emotions may send mixed messages within the context of the same situation. Each person is a blend of multiple personality traits often living an uneasy alliance under the same skin, often conflicting. For this reason, you may feel uncertainty. At times, when making decisions, some parts of you may be out of synch, much like an instrument out of tune in an orchestra or a splash of color that doesn't fit.

Your ability to go wholeheartedly for an outcome and therefore make powerful decisions, and even—once you have made a decision—to focus your attention, may be radically affected by how you reconcile and creatively manage these different parts of yourself. It is rare to be able to

The Principle of Relevance

be completely and congruently decisive in relation to a certain outcome. The bigger the stakes at play, and the larger the outcome, the more parts of oneself will be drawn into the decision-making process and the greater the possibility of internal incongruity and conflicting purposes will be.

The most effective way to build internal power in one's attention, focus, and decision making is to refine one's self-knowledge. Self-knowledge allows an individual to identify the incongruities in himself or herself and acknowledge them. Once those incongruities are acknowledged and understood, it is possible to move past them and focus one's decisions and attention with directness.

The Principle of Relevance

Chapter 3 – Snapshot

- When the brain is overloaded with data, it tends to cut down on data gathering, jump to rapid conclusions, and respond to data immediately as they come, in an unconscious attempt to put an end to the data overload.

- The principle of relevance consists of expanding the amount of information you are able to let in, while at the same time being able to invest the right amount of energy in the right place at the right time, eliminating the unnecessary, responding only to what is relevant, and seeing the big picture with a strong awareness of priorities.

- To master the principle of relevance, you have to work with the following elements:

1. Clarity of purpose

Set a clear purpose to your actions. Become aware of your options and hidden goals and then make a conscious choice about which among them is your priority. Once you have set your purpose, you need to (1) decide on an evidence procedure—how will you know if your outcome meets your values?—and (2) notice what feedback you are getting to assess whether you are going in the right direction.

2. Situational awareness

Situational awareness is the ability to create, acknowledge, and understand a comprehensive and coherent situational representation of an existing situation, which is not static, but rather, continuously updated in accordance with the results of recurrent situation assessments. It is the ability to maintain a constant, clear mental picture of relevant information and its interactions within a complex, dynamic environment. Situational awareness has three stages: perception, comprehension, and projection.

3. Pattern recognition

Pattern recognition involves becoming skilled at seeing the raw data in all their volume and chaotic naturalness and infer from those data the patterns that lie underneath. The ability to see and perceive patterns takes time and effort to be developed; however, once refined, it allows

The Principle of Relevance

fast awareness and decisions based on an instant ability to recognize assonance or dissonance of patterns.

4. Attention

Attention is the process of selection of certain bits of information from the potential millions of bits available. The shape and content of your life depends on how you use your attention: entirely different realities emerge, depending on how it is invested. Paying attention involves energy and mindfulness, and it is the mind's most powerful tool.

5. Self-knowledge and self-mastery

The value of refined situational awareness, pattern recognition skills, and attention is magnified if they are linked to knowledge of the way one reacts to that situation. Self-knowledge allows the identification of incongruities in one's values, thoughts, and feelings. By knowing yourself, you learn to work within your strengths, limitations, and incongruities, thus building internal power in your attention, focus, and decision making.

The Principle of Relevance

PART II

TRAINING YOUR BRAIN TO RECOGNIZE RELEVANCE

We are what we repeatedly do; excellence then is not an act but a habit.

Aristotle

The Principle of Relevance

Introduction to Part II

We are now moving on to the practical part of the book. Part II includes tools that will enable you to work on developing and fine-tuning your ability to work with the *principle of relevance*. We will expand on the concepts described in chapter 3—clarity of purpose, situational awareness, pattern discernment, attention, and self-knowledge and self-mastery—by exploring exercises aimed at developing the skill sets discussed earlier and which, if practiced regularly, will open you to the full expression and application of the *principle of relevance*.

By using the exercises in this chapter, you can train your brain to operate according to the *principle of relevance* in every situation that entails judgment. Discerning relevance among an overload of data and taking action accordingly will then become an automatic process. The principle can be applied to any situation, whether a substantial, long-term project or a small and short-lived personal research project.

If you find that the tools provided in Part II are not engaging for you, you may certainly create your own tools to follow through on the application of the *relevance* principle based on the seeds I have planted in Part I.

If, however, you choose to work with the Relevance Tools, you may find that if you work consistently with them and train yourself to use them habitually and instinctively, you will start processing information more quickly: this will enhance your ability to spot alternatives, expand your options, work with context, and find a quicker and better way to reach your intended goal, whatever that might be, while navigating through different layers of data input.

My advice is to choose a few areas to which you want to apply the *principle of relevance* and go through the exercises one by one, until the process becomes natural to you, until you master it. Then, go back and adapt the tools to your brain processes so that they serve you in the best possible way: play with them, add to them, fine tune them and create new formulas.

As with anything, persistence is key. Though any moment in time is not significant enough to determine the final outcome of a situation, and anything that happens is a long-standing combination of events and situations, it is cultivated behaviors, those we deliberately practice, that tend to manifest themselves repeatedly in both significant and insignificant situations.

Your habits rule the way you actually process information. By using the Relevance Tools © you will train yourself to be aware of what these processes are and then develop or refine your relevance cognition skills. With mindful practice, you will develop new habits and responses. They will become unconscious processes that will sustain your toward an enhanced ability to process information, unleashing in you a higher level of freedom to perceive choices and select opportunities.

FOUR

Principle 1—Clarity of Purpose

Before you begin any project, it is important to arrive at clarity of purpose. This involves developing an unambiguous purpose, chosen from a full set of possible purposes; establishing criteria that will enable you to determine when you have attained your purpose and met your goal; and defining and gathering the resources necessary to reach your goal. These essential first steps are discussed in more detail in the following sections.

1. Clarify Your Purpose

Whatever you do, whether related to a clear-cut end goal, such as completing a project, or a general life purpose, such as bringing joy to people around you, you must have a clear idea in mind of what it is that you want to achieve. Simply to take action without clarity of purpose will create desultory, random outcomes. Rather, ask yourself, what do you want to achieve with your actions? In what way do you want your actions to affect the people and environment around you? In other words, what is the purpose of your actions?

Defining an unambiguous purpose, outcome, or goal involves three steps: (1) acknowledging the purpose of options available to you, (2) choosing a clear and unambiguous purpose, and (3) using your representational systems to imagine yourself being on purpose. These steps are discussed in more detail in the following paragraphs.

The Principle of Relevance

Step 1—Acknowledge the Variety of Options That Are Available to You

Stretch your imagination. Do not overlook anything at first. Think, dream, brainstorm, imagine, write, and discuss with someone the question, what are your options? Is there something you have not considered? Is there another possibility?

What resources do you have available, and how can they help you to clarify your options? How can you break the larger idea down to define possible goals and purposes, and which is most important to you relative to the idea as a whole?

This must be a fully creative explorative process. To kick-start this process, you can also use the mind mapping exercise described in Relevance Tool N. 3, later on in this chapter.

For example, the owner of a small information technology (IT) business, whose core business is developing and operating innovative IT systems for the media industry, might want to increase the scale of the company's operations during the next financial year. While the general idea he has in mind is that of "expanding the business," this actually entails a choice between very different options. A few options available to him are as follows: (a) increasing profits, which might involve entering into a short-term but very lucrative contract with a big client; (b) expanding his influence base, which might entail entering into several long-term, although less profitable, client relationships; and (c) expanding market coverage, which might entail dedicating some months to investing in the research and development of new software programs and therefore

The Principle of Relevance

incurring immediate costs as an investment for potential higher profit later on.

Step 2—Choose, among the Available Options, a Specific One

Once you have acknowledged your options, ask yourself, what is the real outcome I want to achieve? What are the possibilities around it? Are you sure that this is really your purpose? Is there anything you can do to make it more specific?

This is the hardest step. You have to make a choice, and often, you will linger on this choice because you will have several different options that you cannot choose because they depend on others or on situations or events that are not in your own, direct control.

You can always change your mind later on (no one prevents you from changing your mind!), but you will limit yourself greatly if you do not make a first choice. If you don't choose your purpose, in the absence of a reason for seeking some particular form of more recondite information, you will not have any reason to move beyond readily accessible inputs. Table 4.1 describes the attributes your purpose should exemplify.

The Principle of Relevance

Table 4.1. Characteristics of purpose

Characteristic	Actions
Positive and specific	State your purpose in specific and positive terms. Avoid expressing your goal in negative terms (such as "avoiding x" or "not becoming x").
Controllable	If your purpose requires someone else to take action, clarify whether it is within your power to influence that person's behavior. If the answer is no, choose a different purpose.
The right size: neither too big nor too small	If your purpose is too big, it will be daunting and a cause of anxiety; if it is too small, it will be boring. If you feel that your purpose might be too ambitious (and you know this by the level of anxiety that you feel when you think about it), break it down into smaller concepts and work on each one at a time. If your purpose, on the other hand, is too small (and you know this if there is nothing about it that excites your interest), you may want to increase the scale of it.

The Principle of Relevance

Step 3—Imagine Yourself Being on Purpose with All Your Representational Systems

Imagine the result you want as if you had already achieved it, in all its detail and using all your representational systems: visual (sight), auditory (sound), kinesthetic (touch/feeling), or even smell and taste. Neurolinguistic programming authors have published a vast array of work relating to representational systems, which can help you discover which is your predominant or preferred system and how to develop your weaker systems (for a few examples, see the section on neurolinguistic programming in the bibliography).

According to this work, we use our senses outwardly to perceive the world and inwardly to represent the experience to ourselves.[11] Each one of us has a preferred representational system (either visual, auditory, kinesthetic, or, usually to a lesser degree, olfactory and gustatory) through which we learn processes and remember information. This internal preference affects our perceptions, memories, and the language we use to describe our experiences to others. It is therefore extremely valuable to learn to recognize your own preferred representational system so that you can train your brain to represent the end result that you are seeking in the manner that is most effective and impactful.

---

[11] Joseph O'Connor and John Seymour, *Introducing NLP* (Element, 2002).

2.   Set Out Evaluation Criteria

Criteria are values that are important in a given context. You will not know whether you are on the path of relevance if you do not define measurable criteria that need to be met for you to perceive you are on track.

The kind of criteria (whether objective or dependent on another person's feedback) you want to work toward are in and of themselves often unimportant and greatly depend on the outcome you want to achieve. The criteria must have a symbolic message for you: that you have succeeded in your purpose. This knowledge creates order in consciousness and strengthens your will to stay on purpose.

In the absence of a paradigm, all the facts that could possibly pertain to achieving any given purpose are likely to seem equally relevant. Certain purposes, for example, involving material goals, will be easier to pair with objective criteria, whereas others will give you a harder time. If you are learning to drive a car, planning flights for a holiday, or desire to buy a house on the beach, you will be able to set down certain specific criteria rather easily; on the other hand, if your purpose is to write an article or a book, the criteria will be more subjective. If your purpose is intellectual or spiritual, your evaluation criteria will depend entirely on your sensibility. In each and every case, you will be able to define at least two or three clear evaluation criteria.

Your criteria need to meet the following parameters:

The Principle of Relevance

- They need to be specific and measurable.

- They need to be positive.

- They need to be controllable.

For example, if you are a small business owner and, after evaluating your options, you choose an immediate increase in profit for the current financial year as your purpose, your criteria will be objective and financially based. If, however, your purpose is to write a research paper on a determined subject, some of the criteria will be objective and may be given by someone else (How long does the paper need to be? Does it need to be written in a certain style or from a certain perspective?), and some of the criteria will be subjective and based on your own sensibility and preferences. For example, some of your subjective criteria could be as follows:

1. the paper discusses at least four mainstream theories on the subject

2. the paper includes a discussion of at least one original idea or original interpretation or application of an existing idea

3. the information is presented consistently, and it has an introduction and a conclusion

4. the language is fluent and presents no apparent ambiguities or obscurities

You may list as many criteria as you want, and it is useful at first to brainstorm as many as you can and then trim them down to a maximum of

The Principle of Relevance

five or six of which you can keep track and to which you can be certain to adhere.

It is very important not to make the mistake of confusing your criteria with your purpose! The criteria are not your purpose; rather, they are measurable evaluation parameters through which you will check that you are on track with the purpose you have chosen.

For the criteria to work for you, you must frequently check them and make small corrections to your course, as necessary, to get back on track. You should also, to the extent possible, maintain your criteria throughout the process, without heeding the temptation to change them. Otherwise, you risk creating a self-defying system of criteria which become impossible to meet.

3. Define Which Resources You Need

Once you have defined your purpose and set out your evaluation criteria, you will be ready to identify both the resources you need to bring about your plan and any limitations you need to take into account and overcome. The resources can be internal, such as specific skills or states of mind, or external, such as information, deliverables, and tools.

Remember that there is a key to every door, and clearly identifying your limitations can help you find the key to overcoming them. If a specific limitation is particularly important and, at the same time, particularly difficult to overcome, you can set a small subgoal specifically aimed at overcoming that limitation.

The difficult part about this exercise is recognizing and deciding how much investment, in terms of strength, time, and resources, to devote to a specific task so that you can set boundaries to your effort and use just the right amount of energy and resources.

Relevance Tool N. 1, on the next page, provides a checklist that you can use when defining your purpose and criteria. While completing this exercise may be time consuming at first, with time and repeated use, the organizational purpose of the exercise will become so well incorporated into your routine that it will become automatic and even occur in the background, unconsciously.

Relevance Tool N. 1 – The Outcome Checklist

The Outcome Checklist

1. Clarity of Purpose

Parameter	Core Question		Description	Check when completed
				☐
Positive	What is the positive purpose		Describe it in positive terms	☐
Controllable	Is my purpose within my concern	Yes		☐
		No	Chose a purpose that is controllable and repeat checklist	☐
Specific	Who, where, when, what?		Describe	☐
Size	What is the size of my purpose?	Yes	Continue	☐
	Do I feel comfortable with it? Is it too big (it makes me feel anxious)?	Too Big	Chunk it down into smaller ideas or goals and repeat checklist	☐
	Is it too small (it makes me feel bored)?	Too small	Enlarge, think bigger and repeat check list	

The Principle of Relevance

The Outcome Checklist			

2. Set out evaluation criteria

Parameter	Core Question	Description	Check when completed
Evidence	How will I know I am on purpose? What are my objective parameters	Describe it in positive terms	☐
Experience	What will the sensory based experience be: What will I see? What will I feel? What will I hear?	Describe it in positive terms	☐

The Principle of Relevance

3. Limitations and Resources

Parameter	Core Question		Description	Check when completed
Resources	What tools resources do I need?	Internal? Skills, state of mind	Describe it in positive terms	☐
		External? Information, deliverables, support from people etc	Describe it in positive terms	☐
	What do I need to do to obtain these resources?	Internal? Skills, state of mind	Describe it in positive terms	☐
		External? Information, deliverables, support from people etc	Describe it in positive terms	☐
Limitations	What limitations do I have?		Describe it in positive terms	☐
	What do I need to do to overcome them?		Describe it in positive terms	☐

The Principle of Relevance

Relevance Tool N. 1 – Example

The IT business owner, for example, after evaluating his options, may have decided that his purpose for the next financial year is to raise profits by landing a big client contract.

Here is how the outcome checklist could look on this basis.

1. Clarity of Purpose

Parameter	Core Question		Description	Check when completed
Positive	What is the positive purpose		Acquire a new customer	☐
Controllable	Is my purpose within my concern	Yes	Continue	☐
		No		☐
Specific	Who, where, when, what?		Who: television broadcasting company intending to explore in new media What: Looking for IT systems developer or R&D platform in Asia When: end of the year	☐
Size	What is the size of my purpose?	Yes	Continue	☐
	Do I feel comfortable with it? Is it too big (it makes me feel anxious)?	Too Big		☐
	Is it too small (it makes me feel bored)?	Too small		☐

83

The Principle of Relevance

The small business owner scenario applied to
The Outcome Checklist

2. Set out evaluation criteria

Parameter	Core Question	Description	Check when completed
Evidence	How will I know I am on purpose? What are my objective parameters	Contract signed First deposit paid	☐
Experience	What will the sensory based experience be: What will I see? What will I feel? What will I hear?	Contract for at least [x] USD amount The client says to me "that's exactly the partnership we were looking for" I feel energetic and expansive	☐

The Principle of Relevance

3. Limitations and Resources

Parameter	Core Question		Description	Check when completed
Resources	What tools resources do I need?	Internal? Skills, state of mind	Positive, entrepreneurial, proactive, aggressive, professional, creative	☐
		External? Information, deliverables, support from people etc	Dedicated and professional team, people networks, information on expansion plans of market players/potential client targets, stronger office in Hong Kong and new office in Europe	☐
	What do I need to do to obtain these resources?	Internal? Skills, state of mind	Hire a coach? Build professional skills such as sales Find time by prioritizing and delegating	☐
		External? Information, deliverables, support from people etc	Networking Conversations Research Government institutions official reports Internet research Training stronger team to take over operations	☐
Limitations	What limitations do I have?		Weak internal team Weak office in Hong Kong Undecided office manager in Europe	☐
	What do I need to do to overcome them?		Motivate office manager Train internal team Implement MIS (management information systems)	☐

85

The Principle of Relevance

FIVE

Principle 2—Situational Awareness

Once you have gained a clear understanding of your purpose, take time to notice and understand your surroundings, whether physical or cognitive. In other words, perform a situational analysis. Start off by collecting the data you possess that relate to the purpose, topic, or issue with which you want to deal, and from there, look for alternative routes and pathways to gathering more and deeper data. Just collect what you have and initially observe it, suspending judgment and letting the information come to you in a nonlogical manner.

To learn the most from any situation or experience, you will need to gather information from as many points of view as possible. New ideas emerge from viewing the same piece of information from different representational systems and viewpoints.

To be able to do this, you have to make a deliberate choice to overcome the initial instinct to block data flow to avoid overload by responding immediately and let data flow to you without, initially, taking any action.

As we have seen in chapter 3, situational awareness is the emergence of meaning along a gradient of complexity. Situational awareness evolves along three gradients: perception, comprehension, and projection.

86

The cognitive capabilities involved in the three stages of situational awareness—perception, comprehension, and projection—are summarized in Table 5.1 and discussed in detail in subsequent sections. Each of the comprehension and projection stages involves elements of pattern recognition. As I have discussed elsewhere, pattern recognition is an extremely important cognitive skill, and therefore it will be discussed separately in chapter 6.

Table 5.1. Three stages of situational awareness

Skill	Capability	Tools
1. Perception	Noticing	Relevance Tool N. 2 -Perception: recognizing data relevance
2. Comprehension	Context	Relevance Tool N. 3 - The Context Chart: recognizing context
	Pattern recognition elements (discussed in chapter 6):	
	– logical	Relevance Tool N. 4 - The Baconian Pattern Chart
	– intuitive	Relevance Tool N. 5 -Traditional Mind Mapping Example
3. Projection	Integrating	Relevance Tool N. 6 -Layered Mind Mapping
	Pattern recognition elements (discussed in chapter 6):	
	– sense making	Relevance Tool N. 7 -Multiple Players Mapping
	– future projection	

The Principle of Relevance

1. Perception

Perception involves awareness of the status, attributes, and dynamics of relevant elements in the environment. Perception involves monitoring, cue detection, and simple recognition to build awareness of multiple situational elements (objects, events, people, systems, environmental factors) and their current states (locations, conditions, modes, actions).

For example, imagine that you have been placed in charge of forming a committee to gather information about the sales procedures of your company, with the end result being the in-house publication of sales manuals for new employees. Use your perception to determine who is available as a potential team member. Of those who are available, what tasks can each perform best, and what information can each supply with expertise? How much time do you have, and how long will it take to collaborate to form the final manual? What tasks can be performed concurrently with others?

You may work on heightening your perception skills when evaluating information by working with Relevance Tool N. 2. The purpose of Relevance Tool N. 2 is to train yourself to assess relevance and increase your perception levels so that you become skilled at assessing the relevance of a large quantity of multilayered data.

Whenever you encounter a piece of data, you may assess its relevance to your purpose by positioning the data on the chart based on the two parameters of "On Purpose" and "Significant." Your data will be relevant only if they are both highly significant and on purpose.

Relevance Tool N. 2 – The Perception Chart—Recognizing Data Relevance

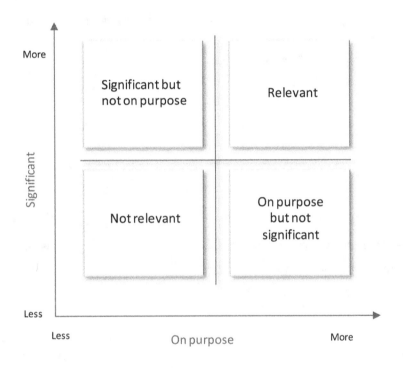

The Principle of Relevance

On Purpose

Refers directly to your purpose: the goal you want to achieve or issue you are dealing with

Is of interest to your purpose

Contains sources of reference

Significant

Qualified

Solves a problem

Gives a particular insight

Is referred to by several other sources

Gives a competitive advantage

Moves you forward

Relevance Tool N. 2 – Example

In the IT business owner scenario, after the IT business owner has chosen his intended purpose, that is the right time to apply situational awareness skills to understand what is going on in the market.

In terms of perception, he needs to acquire information about the market and who his potential clients could be. He will gain information from a number of sources: direct enquiries, Internet research, and word of mouth. He will gain information as to what his competitors have done, what potential clients have done, how the market is responding, and what his suppliers think.

Through his enquiries and research, the entrepreneur may obtain the following information:

1. An MBA classmate is COO of a major market player (the "Potential Client") in Europe.
2. One of his existing clients tells you that the Potential Client intends to expand its distribution operations in China.
3. The Potential Client is asking questions about IT outsourcing in China.
4. An Internet search reveals that cost of labor in Eastern Europe has gone up.
5. The Potential Client is partially running IT operations in China, but the development projects are not progressing well.
6. Statistics from the trade commission show an increase in technology deals in China.
7. A friend tells him that the European CTO of the Potential Client is going to be let go for delocalization purposes.

He may then evaluate the information you have received through Relevance Tool N. 2 . This is what it could look like.

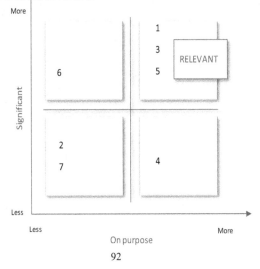

The Principle of Relevance

2. Comprehension

Comprehension is the meaning of the pieces of data you have gathered as integrated with each other and in terms of your purpose. It is the "so what" of the data you have collected.

As discussed in chapter 3, this level involves a synthesis of disjointed perception elements through the processes of context and pattern recognition, interpretation, and evaluation. At this level, you will interpret and integrate data to understand how they will impact your goals and objectives. This includes developing a comprehensive picture of the situation being analyzed or of that portion of the situation of concern to you.

Data integration is achieved by understanding context. Understanding a situation in context will help you get clarity on how the data available to you play out together with the current dynamics and forces of the environment, the complexity of relationships, and roles of human emotions. This will train you to see situations from every perspective, allowing you to adapt to various unpredictable situations.

First, look at the content: what is this piece of data? What is it called? What does it look like?

Then the context: what does this piece of data mean? How does it relate to others? Is it similar or different? Where and how does it fit into the system? Nearly all information and behaviors are useful somewhere, but it all depends on context.

Exercise your context awareness by working the information you have gathered with Relevance Tool N. 3. Take the raw data that are available to you and feed them into the chart.

The purpose of this tool is to train your brain to recognize quickly the role that contextual elements play in the overall result. Does anything change when you alter one of the elements in the context chart? Is a different result produced? Again, learning to use this tool automatically in a linear situation allows you to apply it quickly in multilayered, complex situations.

Relevance Tool N. 3 – The Context Chart—Recognizing Context

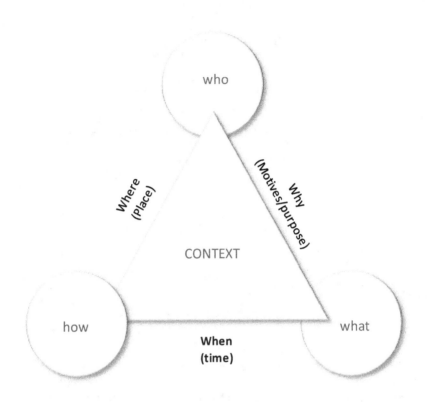

who

Where
(Place)

Why
(Motives/purpose)

CONTEXT

how

what

When
(time)

The Principle of Relevance

Relevance Tool N. 3 – Example

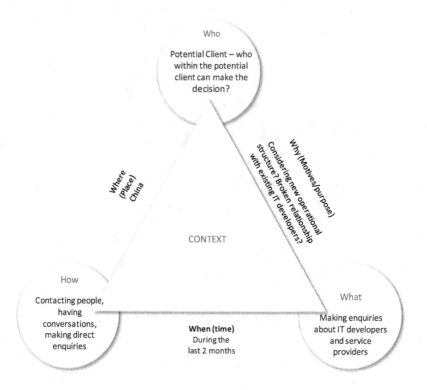

The IT business owner, for example, after having collected all information available and having assessed its relevance through Relevance Tool N. 2, would need to comprehend that information by putting it into context.

He can do so by taking the relevant information in the upper right quadrant of Relevance Tool N. 2 and inserting it in Relevance Tool N. 3. The exercise would look as follows.

Example: A key element in this chart is the "Where" – China. If a competitor located in India contacts the potential client and shows them a good case for IT outsourcing in India, the potential client's attention might shift and your business opportunity stall. A second key element is the "Who" – Potential Client. Who is the actual decision maker within the client organization and how does that change your approach? Is your MBA contact the decision maker or is he simply a gateway?

The Principle of Relevance

3. Projection

The third and highest level of situational awareness involves the ability to project the future actions of the elements in the environment. Projection is achieved through perception and knowledge of the status and dynamics of the elements, comprehension of the situation (through context and pattern recognition), and then projection of this information forward in time to determine how it will affect the future.

Projection involves the ability to make a dynamic mental representation of the situation and combine it with temporal and spatial components. As new inputs enter the system, the individual incorporates them into this mental representation, making changes, as necessary, in plans and actions to achieve desired goals.

As the ability to project is highly dependent on the ability to see patterns, I refer the reader to chapter 6, which deals specifically with pattern discernment, and its accompanying relevance tools.

SIX

Principle 3—Pattern Discernment

1. Introduction

Situational awareness is greatly enhanced by the ability to recognize patterns of key factors in the environment. Recognizing patterns is a skill that can be developed with regular practice, and it is very fulfilling to the brain ("aha" moments are usually a result of discovery of a pattern).

The learning of a new language is a very common situation involving an exercise bank that automatically forces us to improve our pattern discernment abilities. After you have learned enough of the language to be able to follow a conversation or read a simple book, you will only be successful at accessing the next step of language learning if you stop paying attention to the meaning of each word taken separately and instead seek to understand the overall meaning of a sentence. Often, by doing this, you begin to fill in the blanks of the meanings of those words you do not understand completely, and slowly, you start recognizing the patterns of the language, its DNA.

Other than in the context of learning a new language, you can choose to deliberately apply the same principles whenever you are dealing with a new situation. Pattern discernment is essential to the skill of projection. In

The Principle of Relevance

the following sections, I present general frameworks for understanding and developing pattern discernment skills.

2.   Pattern Recognition 1—The Logical Way

Relevance Tool N. 4—The Baconian Method

This is an inductive-logical method of pattern analysis, which I will call the "Baconian method" because it was described by Francis Bacon in his 1620 philosophical work *The Novum Organon*. This method is a simple but very effective tool to help kick-start your pattern recognition habits. It consists of drawing a list of all situations in which a given thing (phenomenon, information, situation, etc.) you are analyzing occurs as well as a list of situations in which it does not occur. Then you rank your lists according to the degree to which the thing you are analyzing occurs in each one. On this basis, you should be able to deduce what factors match the occurrence of the phenomenon in one list and don't occur in the other list, and also what factors change in accordance with the way the data had been ranked.

You can work with the Baconian pattern chart by analyzing a given situation as follows:

1. *Presence column.* List here all the cases wherein the phenomenon exists.

2. *Absence column.* List here all the cases in which the phenomenon under analysis does not appear to be present.

3. *Degree variance column*. List here the increase and decrease of the given phenomenon in one situation or different situations.

Relevance Tool N. 4 – The Baconian Pattern Chart

Description of the phenomenon you are analyzing: When does the potential client respond favorably to me?		
The table of Presence : When does it occur?	Table of Absence: When does it not occur?	Table of Degrees: What makes it occur in lesser or higher degree?
Describe situation	Describe situation	Assess degree: Describe situation
Describe situation	Describe situation	Assess degree: Describe situation
Describe situation	Describe situation	Assess degree: Describe situation

103

Relevance Tool N. 4 – Example

Relevance Tool N. 4 can be applied to each and every recurring situation in life, including behavior patterns in personal relationships or scientific phenomena.

In the IT business owner situation, on the basis of the information he has collected, analyzed, and put into context, he has decided to pursue a specific client who could be interested in his services. Before he submits an official proposal to the client or enters into official negotiations, he may want to map out the recurring patterns in his relationship with the potential client. This would be ideally done when he has a relationship history with that client, but can be done also on the basis of limited exchanges and data. He could try to verify when the client responds favorably to him so that the best possible offer can be prepared. In order to do so, he could go through the exchange of e-mails with that potential client and try to sort out a recurring pattern.

Bacon himself, however, warns against a delusion which he calls *Idola Tribus* (Idols of the Tribe): this is the human tendency to perceive more order and regularity in systems than truly exists and is due to people following their preconceived ideas. For this reason, logical-inductive pattern recognition is often more effective if paired up with a more intuitive and creative approach such as mind mapping.

Description of the phenomenon you are analyzing: When does the potential client respond favorably to me?		
The table of Presence : When does it occur?	Table of Absence: When does it not occur?	Table of Degrees: What makes it occur in lesser or higher degree?
When I touch base with them on a regular basis		Higher degree: When my communications are succinct and to the point Lower degree: When I use language that is too sophisticated and literary
When I mention innovative ideas and the ability of my team to have a proactive approach.		Higher degree: when I explain those ideas
When I show understanding of their business, brand, needs and vision for the future	When I don't show commitment and belief in their plans	
When I show professionalism and execution		

105

The Principle of Relevance

3. Pattern Recognition 2—The Creative Way

Relevance Tool N. 5—Traditional Mind Mapping

A *mind map* is a visual diagram used to represent concepts and ideas in a nonhierarchical form. A keyword or picture representing the main issue or idea is drawn or written in the center of a blank page, and then associated ideas, words, or concepts are drawn or written into the map radially around this center node.

By presenting ideas in a radial, graphical, nonlinear manner, mind maps encourage a creative approach to planning and organizational tasks. Though the branches of a mind map represent hierarchical tree structures, their radial arrangement disrupts the prioritizing of concepts typically associated with hierarchies presented with more linear visual cues. The nonhierarchical nature of the mind map allows for the free-flowing, unstructured connection of concepts and therefore facilitates the recognition of relationships and the discernment of patterns.

A mind map is a graphic expression of the natural patterns of the brain as it mirrors the synaptic patterns of the brain cells, which branch out of a center called the nucleus. A mind map (or similar concept, however you may wish to call it) is a tool that can be used to enhance learning, brainstorming, memory, visual thinking, and creative problem solving.

Mind mapping is intuitive, and a number of philosophers, artists, and thinkers have made consistent use of it in the past. In recent years, psychologist and author Tony Buzan popularized mind mapping in a

The Principle of Relevance

number of books and educational programs,[12] and numerous writers have referred to Buzan's works.

As a starting point for traditional mind mapping, begin your map with a symbol or picture representing the topic you want to explore at the center of your page, and then freely unfold associations from it. From each association, you can also create a submap or a separate map. You may use words, but also pictures and symbols or a combination of both, depending on your preferred representational system.

Following is an example of how mind mapping helped me unfold some of the ideas included in this book and find the underlying pattern in the idea of relevance that gave the book its title.

---

[12] See, in particular, Tony Buzan, *The Mind Map Book* (http://www.buzanworld.com).

The Principle of Relevance

Relevance Tool N. 5 – Traditional Mind Mapping

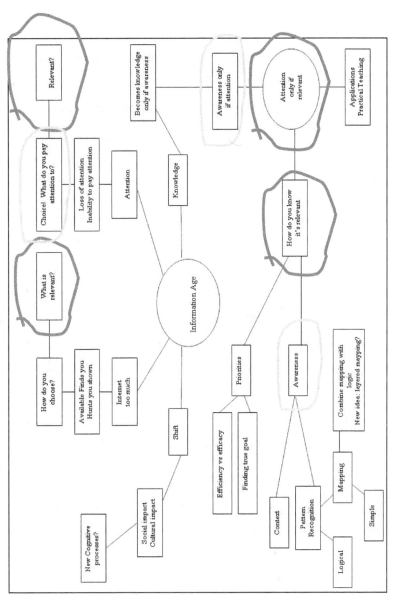

The Principle of Relevance

4. Projecting Ideas into the Future

Relevance Tool N. 6—Layered Mind Mapping

The traditional mind mapping exercise presented earlier has a missing element: the temporal factor. Traditional mind mapping is essentially time flat. You can take mind mapping a step further by applying a system I will call *layered mapping*. I developed layered mapping to address situations that require a holistic integration of right-brain thinking with logical, time-oriented left-brain thinking.

This map allows you to track and identify past, present, and future patterns. Begin as in traditional mind mapping by writing or drawing your core idea, issue, or project in the center. Then create three different sections, representing past, present, and future. Keep adding ideas and information in a nonstructured, nonhierarchical way as they come, as in the traditional mind mapping system, but when you write down the ideas, make sure to insert them in the area related to past, present, or future, depending on whether an idea relates to the past, present, or future, respectively. If an idea relates to all three, you may draw a linking line across the three sections. When you have finished, you will be able to see what the patterns are.

If this model does not fit in with your brain's processes, there are other options that you can consider using. Close your eyes and visualize how you normally imagine time. Some people imagine past and future as a line going from left to right; others see it as standing respectively behind them and in front of them. Whatever your vision is, go with it, and use the image that represents your representational system more accurately.

109

You may, at this point, also draw three separate mind maps: one for the past, one for the present, and one for the future. Place the maps together and connect the dots between the elements arising out of the maps that have some element of similarity. Place these new elements into a new mind map and create a new logical-inductive analysis beginning from the similarities and patterns you have found.

Relevance Tool N. 6 – Layered Mind Mapping

TOPIC	PAST	PRESENT	FUTURE

Relevance Tool N. 6 – Example

The IT business owner could use this tool to brainstorm ideas for what future developments can be foreseen in terms of IT platforms for the television industry.

TOPIC	PAST	PRESENT	FUTURE
Ideas for the development of IT platforms for television			
	Linear Fixed content Tailored channels		
		Tailored channels On demand Interactive Feedback Multiple choices Web 2.0 Virtual reality games	
			Virtual reality games Multiple endings possible for a movie? Story created by users? Feedback and choices in a movie or tv program like a videogame

5.   Projecting Actions into the Future

Relevance Tool N. 7—Multiple Players Mapping

The same structure of layered mind mapping can be used for multiple players mapping. Multiple players mapping is a very effective way to analyze, in an integrated way, a situation that involves interconnected events or players, in which every move is dependent on what another person will do first or how a certain event will play out, in the same manner as a game of chess. Though some of the relevance tools we have explored can be done mentally (without an actual paper exercise), once they become second nature, and even mentally applied to multilayered information, when dealing with multiparty scenarios, it is extremely useful to draft an actual scenario plan. When multiple parties are involved, it is in fact often easy to overlook certain potential outcomes or actions that may come to fruition because of two main reasons: (1) multiple parties tend to form coalitions and (2) each party's alternatives and options constantly shift and need to be reassessed based on the other parties' responses.

In the first situation slot, record the situation as it is at the moment when you are looking at it. Then describe the first action taken by the player who has set in motion a change to that situation. In the following "Level" lines, include only events and actions that derive from those included in the preceding line. For example, in the "Level 3" line, only include the actions that are a consequence of the actions that have been listed in the "Level 2" line, and so on. You can add as many levels as you need, depending on the complexity of how the situation may unfold, and

113

as many columns as the number of players. The freedom of this model is that you can add columns and levels if new players are added.

By using these tools, you will be able to find patterns between seemingly unrelated events and actions and build very sharp strategies for dealing with them.

Relevance Tool N. 7 – Multiple Players Mapping

Multiple Players Mapping					
	Player 1	**Player 2**	**Player 3**	**Player 4**	**Player N** (as many as needed)
Level 1	Action 1		Action 2 (simultaneous as action 1)		
Level 2				Action 3	
Level 3		Action 4			
Level 4	Action 5			Action 6	
Level 5			Action 7		
Level N (as many as needed)					
Outcome	Final Result				

Relevance Tool N. 7 – Example

For example, imagine that, being the small business owner who is trying to raise his profits by gaining a new client contract, you find yourself in a complex situation where you are competing with another person or company for the client relationship you are seeking. The potential client lets you know that in order to be sure to land the contract, you need to bring in the services of a particularly visionary and skilled software developer, either as a consultant or employee, who is also, at the same time, being courted by your competitor. You have four main parties here:

1. you
2. the potential client ("Client")
3. the software developer ("Developer")
4. your competitor ("Competitor")

The Developer will agree to work with either You or the Competitor, depending on who lands the contract with the Client. At the same time, the Client will only award the contract to the one who, between You and the Competitor, can guarantee the availability of that particular skill that the Developer has to offer.

In order to decide which actions to take and the potential outcomes, you may want to lay out your situation in a Multiple Players Mapping scenario. When doing so, you should leave space for other factors, perhaps an extra player that you have not thought of at the moment. There could be, for example, an external party who has some kind of influence on either the Client or the Developer (the "Influencer") and you might gain this information or insight only while starting to work with the Multiple Players Mapping. A simplified scenario could look like this. There are four parties, so this could be done with a square; however, I have left a space for the Influencer: there is often in fact in every life situation an unforeseen player who is not known to the parties until very late in the game.

Multiple Players Mapping					
	You	Client	Developer	Influencer	Competitor
Level 1	Engage Developer				
Level 2			Asks for counteroffer from competitor		
Level 3					Informs Client that it is about to strike a deal with Developer
Level 4		Communicates with Influencer			
Level 5				Informs you of Competitor's moves	
Level N (as many as needed)	Choices: engage Developer, use Influencer to affect client etc				
Outcome	Final Result				

117

The Principle of Relevance

SEVEN

Principles 4 and 5—Attention and Self-Knowledge

Using the skills and exercises described in the previous chapters, you have defined your purpose with clarity; following this, you have performed a situational analysis, and through that, you have collected data, analyzed them, comprehended them, and integrated them. The final step is making a decision on if, how, and when to respond to information you have received, collected, analyzed for relevance, comprehended, and integrated. If and how to respond is key to the relevance principle, and it is determined using the skills of attention and self-knowledge/self-mastery. This is where you make your decisions, taking in the information that is relevant to your purpose (attention) but acting only based on a deliberate choice and not on impulse (self-knowledge/self-mastery).

1. Attention

Merriam-Webster's Collegiate Dictionary defines attention as "(a) the act or state of . . . applying the mind to an object of sense or thought; (b) a condition of readiness for such attention involving especially a selective narrowing or focusing of consciousness and receptivity." The *Merriam-Webster* definition interestingly includes reference to *consciousness*. Consciousness itself is defined as "(a) the quality or state of being aware

The Principle of Relevance

especially of something within oneself; (b) the state or fact of being conscious of an external object, state, or fact."

So being attentive means being conscious and being conscious means being aware. Aware of what, exactly? Attention involves clear awareness of what we are thinking, feeling, and doing and therefore knowing what we are doing and why. *Attention* is another word for *mindfulness*.

Think about what happens to your attention when you enter a rage or are swept away by an intense emotion. You lose most of your control and mental capacity. Your emotional outpouring controls your actions, and awareness of what you are doing, and why, is temporarily suspended.

When a person is able to channel, clearly and energetically, his or her attention to the activity and situation in which the person finds himself or herself, the person is in a state of perfect awareness. You can fully grasp the importance of attention when you consider how people are subconsciously attracted to individuals who seem to be particularly conscious or who seem to be able to hold a high degree of attention, and how people tend to shy away from those who seem to have a lesser degree of attention.

Think of a surgeon performing open-heart surgery, a symphony orchestra conductor, or a jet pilot. None of these extremely sophisticated activities, in which the slightest error or lapse of attention could dramatically alter the overall outcome (with life-and-death consequences in the case of the surgeon and the jet pilot), could be performed without the highest possible level of attention.

The Principle of Relevance

So by attention, I refer to the ability to be highly aware, and therefore in control of, thoughts, feelings, and actions. When you are in a state of attention, you know what you are doing and why you are doing it.

Using multiple players mapping, the multiparty situation in which the IT business owner is striving for a business contract requires the business owner, to master the situation, to exhibit a high level of attention to

1. his thoughts: what he rationally believes he should do

2. his feelings: anger, fear, competition

3. the situation: each and every other person's thoughts, feelings, and actions and the dynamics of the whole situation

4. his options, as they become apparent as the situation evolves

5. his purpose

So what does paying attention involve? What does it trigger? What does it require of us? How can we learn to do it?

Your thoughts and feelings usually dominate your perceptions of the outer world and trigger your actions. Becoming familiar with what your senses are conveying from the outer world, the content of your mind (your thoughts), and the flow of your emotions is the first step to mastering your attention.

My suggestion therefore is to work on sharpening your attention by taking up a regular practice of meditation. There are many different

The Principle of Relevance

schools of meditation employing different techniques and you can read more about it my book *Meditation For Busy Minds*.

Generally, however, they all practice mental exercises aimed at harnessing the ever changing, ever shifting power of your mind by developing focused attention. Attention essentially develops in three stages.

Concentration

Concentration is the ability to center your mind on whatever you wish to direct it to. The essential idea is to hold the concentration or focus of attention in one direction. This is not the forced concentration of, for example, solving a difficult mathematics problem; rather, it is a form closer to the state of mind that could be called *receptive concentration*. Concentration involves focusing the mind in one direction, instead of letting it radiate out in a million different directions.

Contemplation

Contemplation is the ability to direct your consciousness to explore any chosen object or idea in profound depth. In contemplation, the mind is able to differentiate between the perceiver, the means of perception, and the objects perceived; between words, their meanings, and ideas; and at the same time, viewing them as fused in an undifferentiated continuum. In contemplation, the mind is connected with the object of attention; there is a sense of being "one with" the object or activity that is the focus of attention.

121

Continuation

Continuation is a peak state of attention that enables you to move beyond concentration and contemplation into an uninterrupted period of absorption in the awareness of the moment. When you succeed in becoming so absorbed in something that your mind becomes completely one with it, you are in a state of continuation.

Relevance Tool N. 8 – The Attention Exercise

A simple exercise to work on your concentration is to spend some time every day focusing on a single inanimate object.

This may be a lit candle or a simple colorful object, such as an apple. Place it in front of you and look at it for a few minutes. Then close your eyes and hold the image in your mind for 10 to 15 minutes. Hold it there, in your mind's eye and focus only on that image: see its colors and shape, sense its texture, and smell its scent.

Don't strain; don't try too hard. Maintain your focus even if your concentration or your meditation object flies away at times.

Continue gathering and refocusing your attention on your meditation object.

Enjoy the process. Let your ability for attention develop: it will become progressively stronger with regular practice.

2. Self-Knowledge/Self-Mastery

Self-knowledge and self-mastery are perhaps the most important aspects of finding relevance. This involves becoming a master of yourself and responsible for yourself, so that you are able to recognize and deliberately decide when to act and when not to act, and with how much strength. By being, at all times, the master of your own mind, you may let other people advise you, and you may always keep your mind open to interesting information, however you make your own final decisions. As simple as this principle sounds, rest assured that you need your full awareness switched on at all times to live by it.

As discussed under "Attention," meditation techniques can greatly help you achieve this state of mental independence and sharpen your focus and your attention to levels of depth unimaginable for the uninitiated.

Throughout this book, I have discussed the importance of attention, self-knowledge, and self-mastery as essential to finding relevance. These can be gained by action and reflection, or ideally, by both. Most of us have become very accomplished at action; we have been given lectures on leadership skills; and we have been trained to become goal oriented and practical. However, activity alone is not sufficient. Our minds and our bodies cannot grow, develop, and learn to draw order from chaos without allowing for time to get away from the hustle and bustle of the torrential stream of activities, stimuli, and thoughts to which we are constantly subjected.

Most people act compulsively; most of the time, they are not aware of what they are doing, let alone what they are thinking. Once you have mastered attention by being aware of your surroundings, thoughts, and emotions, your actions should reflect your heightened level of attention and awareness.

Self-mastery means being alert to your outcome and keeping your senses open so that you notice what you are getting at any given time. It also means being able to shift your direction, and even your priorities, if necessary, until you are right on track.

Train yourself to use techniques that are fixed means; be prepared to vary them or abandon them and use others if you feel that they are more effective in reaching the desired outcome.

Be prepared to take form in response to the infinite variety of circumstances: let yourself go with the flow and be open to options, possibilities, and opportunities. Be ready for the unexpected; be ready to be confronted with things that don't go as planned; and be flexible. Build mastery of change: be ready to let your brain be surprised by a piece of information that you hadn't thought about, be prepared to adjust your strategy to the situation, and never follow set rules. Be a master of your own mind.

The Principle of Relevance

PART III

THE PRINCIPLE OF RELEVANCE APPLIED TO ORDINARY LIFE

The significant problems we face cannot be solved at the same level of thinking we were at when we created them.

Albert Einstein

127

The Principle of Relevance

EIGHT

Technology Tools and the Overload Factor

We have seen in chapter 1 how most people get overwhelmed and stuck by an overflowing stream of information and requests delivered by telephone, e-mail, and text message. You spend your time on your BlackBerry checking e-mails, even while walking down the street. We have certainly noticed how constantly receiving and responding to e-mails will interrupt work: checking e-mail as it comes in, and thereby letting it become a distraction and interrupt your flow of concentrated work, interferes with focus, and the effect of a lack of focus is that work, even the most basic task, takes more time than it should to be completed.

Notice how long it takes you to shift from one task to the other. What people usually don't notice is that shifting to one activity from another requires a buffer time, which can be as long as fifteen minutes.

The problem is even deeper with portable technology tools. Many people who use a BlackBerry or another high-tech mobile phone with an e-mail push function or other similarly functioning technology tool cannot seem to get their attention away from it; every message received seems urgent and requires immediate attention and an immediate reply, therefore generating more and more messages. People go to meetings and spend their time responding to BlackBerry messages. They have dinner with

The Principle of Relevance

their spouses and spend their time responding to BlackBerry e-mails. Most of the e-mail exchanges are, on second glance, avoidable, unnecessary. Ten e-mails can be exchanged during a family dinner on an issue which would have been solved in five minutes on the phone or with one thought-through, comprehensive e-mail during normal work hours the next day.

Have you ever attended a meeting in which many of the participants are constantly checking their BlackBerry messages? They are not engaged in the meeting. Though there is an impression of great productivity, the productivity level is actually very low. It is hard enough for any person to be a good listener without additional distractions.

As we have seen in previous chapters, mastering the relevance principle involves learning how to disengage from distractions and concentrate attention on a single activity. We can become deliberate in our actions, by hijacking our natural tendency to respond automatically to everything that comes along.

Technology tools are supposed to make us more productive and efficient. Yet being subjected to a continuous torrent of information does nothing but create the anxiety that something is being missed unless answered immediately.

You can realize the impact of this just by looking around. People write e-mails and messages all the time to fill up time perceived as "empty," when they are waiting in a line or for a taxi. However, those "empty times" are the times when the brain processes information in a nonlogical way, creating new solutions and coming up with the most brilliant answers.

These are simmering moments, during which your brain blends in thoughts and information in surprising ways.

If all you do is reply to e-mails, you do not allow your brain to unplug from the ongoing demands of the moment and will fail to see the holistic picture. Although not responding immediately may seem to make you less productive, in truth, the time spent fantasizing, thinking, categorizing, and organizing information freely in your mind, in other words, *finding relevance*, will reward you with efficacy. A thought-through plan or answer is worth a lot more than ten efficiently written but ultimately redundant e-mails, which keep adding to the loop of information exchange without leading to an effective course of action.

If you pay attention, and are honest with yourself as to how you respond to e-mails, you will notice that most e-mails are exchanged with the mere intent of replying, and therefore showing the client, boss, colleague, and so on that you are there and on the job, rather than actually communicating something of value.

I am not suggesting that we abandon our technology tools. They are indeed great tools, provided that they are used correctly. Otherwise, the tools we think are making us more productive can rob us of concentration, harm relationships, and keep us from focusing on critical tasks.

Using technology tools effectively can be done by applying the relevance principle.

Clarity of Purpose

Whenever you feel like responding immediately to an e-mail, go back to the purpose you have set. Does answering meet that purpose? Is it effective to this purpose? Remember that the key is not only doing what is relevant to effectively reach that purpose, but also not doing anything that isn't relevant, so that you can use that energy, space, and time to dedicate your attention to something else. Work with the relevance principle: is the content of this e-mail relevant to effectively reaching your ultimate goal? Does it add content that is of real value, or do you feel the need to answer it merely to show your intent to communicate? What are you taking attention away from if you decide to answer the e-mail?

Be a Master of Your Own Mind

To keep e-mail from interfering with your ability to focus and get things done, try to develop a reasonable time interval for checking e-mail, given your responsibilities. Force yourself to create an e-mail policy for your work. Many lawyers with whom I have worked during my career have told me that it is difficult not to respond to e-mails immediately because they have spoiled their clients, supervisors, and peers by developing the habit of immediate response. If they don't respond almost instantaneously, the sender wonders whether there is an issue or immediately complains.

However, if your response time is immediate, you will be continually distracted. Yes, you will get through your e-mails faster, but what else will you have accomplished?

Breaking habits requires significant effort, but it can be done. It requires discipline, vision, and self-mastery. Dealing with pressing matters as they come, managing day-to-day situations to reach maximum productivity, gives you a sense of immediate satisfaction and makes you feel efficient but, in the long term, often deprives you of vision and efficacy.

The compression created by data overload seems to create a pattern whereby the brain shuts off any creative functioning and proceeds only with logical patterns related to the tasks that it is called to perform. Our thought patterns become rigid and repetitive; we think we are innovative and intelligent, though we are merely applying a set of thinking patterns and rules that we have developed over time, without leaving any space for creativity.

To be able to leave space for your mind to apply the tools discussed in this book, you have to give your mind the gift of simmering moments, incubation, moments during which the mind is not stimulated, moments during which you find relevance.

Chapter 8 – Snapshot

- Constantly receiving and responding to e-mails is a distraction and interrupts the flow of concentrated work. As a consequence, work requires more time than it should.

- Mastering the relevance principle involves hijacking the natural tendency to respond automatically to everything that comes along and becoming deliberate in responses.

- People write e-mails and messages to fill up time perceived as "empty," when in fact, those "empty times" are simmering times, when the brain processes information in a nonlogical way, creating new solutions and coming up with the most brilliant answers.

- Not responding right away may, in the immediate moment, seem to make you less productive or less efficient, but eventually, it rewards you with efficacy.

- Using technology tools effectively can be done by applying the relevance principle:

(1) think about clarity of purpose (does answering meet your purpose? is it effective?) and (2) be a master of your own mind (force yourself to create an e-mail policy for your work).

The Principle of Relevance

NINE

The Principle of Relevance Applied to Work—
Effective Team Play

In most systems and organizations, people work not just as individuals, but as members of a team. Working in a team can be very difficult for many people, especially amidst high data processing requirements. Most of us think that we are great team players, when in reality, we aren't. Most people are trained to work well in a situation in which they are dealing with someone more senior or more junior than them, but not when working with someone who is their peer. In the peer situation, people feel threatened and either try to take over, if they are aggressive, or despise the other person's involvement.

A team is not just any group of individuals: a team is a distinguishable set of two or more people who interact dynamically, interdependently, and adaptively toward a common and valued goal, objective, or mission, thereby creating a unique entity separate from the mere sum of its components. Teamwork is hard work and doesn't just happen on its own. It's a process, and through that process, people bring all their personal experience and expertise to the table. Together, they can produce far better results than they could individually.

There are two essential components to teamwork. The first is openness to each other's influences: the capability of inventing new approaches is increased exponentially because of differences. The second is a strong situational awareness. If any one of the team members has poor situational awareness, it can lead to a critical error in performance that can undermine the success of the entire team.

In a team, each member has a subgoal pertinent to his or her specific role that feeds into the overall team goal. Associated with each member's subgoal is a set of information elements about which he or she is concerned. Each team member needs to have a high level of information on those factors that are relevant for his or her job. Needless to say, it is not sufficient for one member of the team to be aware of critical information if the team member who needs that information is not aware of it. However, as the members of a team are essentially interdependent in meeting the overall team goal, some overlap between each member's subgoal and information requirements will be present. For this reason, information elements and related situational awareness requirements are relevant to multiple team members.

A major part of teamwork involves the area in which these situational awareness requirements overlap: the shared information and situational awareness requirements that exist as a function of the essential interdependency of the team members. This subset of information constitutes the essential core of team coordination. That coordination may occur as a verbal exchange, duplication of displayed information, or by some other means.

If two or more members have different assessments of what the shared information and situational awareness requirements should be, they will behave in an uncoordinated or even counterproductive fashion. This becomes a poorly functioning team. A smoothly functioning team is one in which each team member shares a common understanding of the information that needs to be shared and of the situational awareness requirements shared with other team members.

At the opposite end of the spectrum, a team may also function poorly when all information is indiscriminately shared. Not all information needs to be shared, and sharing every detail only creates a great deal of "noise" and information overload, which impairs the team's ability to get the job done because most time is spent sorting through and processing information that is not relevant. Only that information relevant to the specific requirements of each team member is needed.

The performance and effectiveness of the team as a whole, therefore, is dependent on the following:

1. *Individual awareness.* A high level of awareness of each individual team member of the information and aspects of the situation necessary for the job

2. *The relevance principle.* The degree to which the team members know *which information needs to be shared*, including their higher-level

The Principle of Relevance

assessments and projections (usually not otherwise available to fellow team members) and information on team members' task statuses and current capabilities

3. *Shared awareness in accordance with the relevance principle.* A high level of relevant shared awareness between team members consistent with the relevance principle under item 2; this should provide an accurate common operating picture of those aspects of the situation and elements of information that are needed by more or all team members, including the following:

a. the degree to which team members engage in effective processes for sharing information, checking for conflicting information or perceptions, setting up coordination and prioritization of tasks, and strategizing

b. the devices available for sharing information (verbal communication, technology, visual environment, etc.)

c. the degree to which team members possess mechanisms, such as shared mental models of interpretation, that support their ability to interpret information in the same way and make accurate projections regarding each other's actions

It is, of course, tricky to apply this to a situation in which other team members are not skilled to work with relevance. In this case, the team would work best when guided by a team leader who is apt at working with relevance and conveying the principle to other team members.

The ability to work in a team environment, especially in our current age of collaboration, is essential in the workplace. The principle of relevance can foster not only individual effectiveness, but also successful functioning within a team. In the context of an organization, instilling the principle of relevance in employees has the potential to greatly increase effectiveness as well as create a highly cooperative, information-driven work environment.

Chapter 9 – Snapshot

- Most people are trained to work well in a situation in which they are dealing with someone more senior or more junior than them, but not when working with someone who is their peer.

- There are two essential components to teamwork: (1) openness to each other's influence and (2) situational awareness.

- Each team member has a subgoal pertinent to his or her role that feeds into the overall team goal. Associated with the subgoal is a set of information elements with which he or she is concerned.

- Some overlap between each member's subgoal, and therefore information requirements, is present. Team coordination is knowing where these situational awareness requirements overlap.

- In a poorly functioning team, members may have different assessments of what the shared information and situational awareness requirements should be. In a smoothly functioning team, team members share a common understanding of the information that needs to be shared.

- At the opposite end of the spectrum, a team may be poorly functioning, also, when all information is indiscriminately shared.

- The performance and effectiveness of the team as a whole, therefore, is dependent on the following: (1) individual awareness, or each individual member's awareness of his or her information requirements; (2) the relevance principle, or the degree to which the team members know which information needs to be shared; and (3) shared awareness, in accordance with the relevance principle. The shared awareness between team members includes (1) effective processes for sharing information and checking each other for conflicting information; (2) the devices available for sharing information; (3) the degree to which team members possess shared mental models of interpretation that support their ability to interpret information in the same way and make accurate projections regarding each other's actions.

The Principle of Relevance

TEN

The Principle of Relevance Applied to Critical Situation Management

1. How Do You Make a Decision in Critical Times?

After seeing me go through a difficult situation in which I was forced to make a quick decision about two conflicting priorities in an emergency, a good friend recently asked me a very important question: "How did you know what was right at that moment?"

I didn't know what was right at that moment, and in the high emotional state caused by the crisis (a family member had an accident and was hospitalized, while I was dealing with a very stressful work situation abroad), I wasn't in the healthiest mental state to make decisions. However, I followed a principle that I had set for myself in a different time. I chose to give priority to what I knew I would have given priority to if I were asked to make the decision in calm times.

I am sure you have noticed how when a sudden problem or crisis arises, most people seem to become completely unable to deal with it. If you have ever driven on the highway, you will have noticed how most people behave when they miss their exit. They are driving calmly, and all of a sudden, they realize that they are missing their exit and start swerving

140

The Principle of Relevance

dangerously to drive across the lanes to the ramp. The crisis comes up, and they immediately lose their priority, which is to drive safely. The reason is because a clear priority was not set beforehand, in times of calmness. A deliberate, regular, organized revision of one's priorities ensures clarity on what those priorities are in times of emotional turmoil.

2. How Do You Strategize for a Critical Situation?

Once you have your priorities right, relevance applied to situational awareness is the key skill you need to address a critical situation. Being aware of what is happening around you and understanding what the information means to you now, and what you can foresee for the future, is the basis for situational awareness. When people are required to make critical choices—sometimes at a fast pace—the vast majority of errors that occur are a direct result of failures in data intake and situational awareness.

To deal with a critical situation effectively, you have to do scenario planning based on the relevance principle. Once again, go back to your basics: first, identify your focal issue—what is your priority in the critical situation you are facing? Do you have a time frame? Make sure you have clarity about what the priority is first and foremost. Even in the context of a critical situation, you need a clear purpose in mind to act with relevance: is your objective to neutralize the situation? Minimize risk? Create safety for yourself or another? Be emotionally present and supportive for someone? Get practical things done?

Then, gather the best data available from a broad range of sources. Include outlier information and perspectives that are just now appearing on the horizon and that you could not see initially. Again, to the extent possible under the circumstances, let data come to you without attempting to stop their flow.

There are three main categories of data that come into play in a critical situation, as follows:

Driving forces	These are dominant factors in the situation that are often beyond your control, but they shape the broader environment within which you operate. You'll see some of them immediately, almost instinctively, but you could miss others.
Predetermined elements	These scenario factors will inevitably remain the same, no matter which future unfolds. These are constraining factors and slowly changing phenomena.
Critical uncertainties	These are factors whose outcomes are unpredictable but that are most likely to shape your scenarios by changing their nature or direction.

For example, you are watching a friend's child for the afternoon, and the child, while climbing a tree, falls and breaks her leg. Your priority is to get the child to medical personnel as quickly as possible, but you do not

The Principle of Relevance

know the child's medical history, insurance information, or list of allergies. You try calling your friend, but her cell phone line is giving a failure message—the call will not go through.

1. *Driving forces.* This will be the speed at which the ambulance reaches you and the skill of the doctors who will care for the child.

2. *Predetermined elements.* The child is injured; the child is under your temporary care.

3. *Critical uncertainties.* You do not have access to critical information needed to obtain the best care for the child. You need to contact the parent to seek the best care for the child, but the parent's cell phone is malfunctioning. This could be remedied at any moment, and if remedied, your critical uncertainty is solved. If not, your critical dilemma is ongoing, and you will need to make a decision without this information.

Use the data to generate several divergent yet plausible scenarios, each incorporating different assumptions about the nature of the challenges you might face and projecting possible actions into the future. This lets you examine which futures might unfold and anticipate and rehearse possible responses. Relevance Tool N. 6 (Layered Mind Mapping) and Relevance Tool N. 7 (Multiple Players Mapping) are useful tools to help with scenario planning.

Generate at least three distinct possible outcomes and ways to deal with the situation, and then consider each scenario's implications. Which options are sound in which possible futures? Where are they flawed or

The Principle of Relevance

dangerous? Then, make a decision and respond to the scenario you have chosen to pursue, without being driven by anything else that tries to distract your attention.

The Principle of Relevance

Chapter 10 – Snapshot

- When a sudden problem or crisis arises, most people seem to become completely unable to deal with it.

- Almost always, priorities are not clearly set beforehand, in times of calmness. A deliberate, regular, organized revision of one's priorities ensures clarity on what those priorities are in times of emotional turmoil.

- Once priorities are set, relevance applied to situational awareness is the key skill you need to address a critical situation.

- When people are required to make critical choices—sometimes at a fast pace—the vast majority of errors that occur are a direct result of failures in data intake and situational awareness.

- To deal with a critical situation effectively, you have to do scenario planning based on the relevance principle: (1) identify the focal issue and your purpose—what is your priority in the critical situation you are facing?; (2) gather the best data available from a broad range of sources; (3) understand the data, including driving forces, predetermined elements, and critical uncertainties; (4) project, using the data to generate several divergent yet plausible scenarios, each incorporating different assumptions about the nature of the challenges you might face and projecting possible actions into the future; and (5) make a decision.

The Principle of Relevance

ELEVEN

The Principle of Relevance Applied to Enhancing Quality of Life

We have seen in chapter 1 that one of the conditions that triggers an individual's ability to enjoy the activities he or she pursues is that he or she has chosen those activities. When this happens, actions are not random, nor are they the result of outside determining forces. When you have a feeling of ownership in your decisions, you are more strongly dedicated to the purposes you have chosen. Actions are reliable and internally controlled. Furthermore, when you know that your actions are a result of your own choices, you can more easily modify those actions whenever there is no longer a reason for them. This enhances your commitment and consistency as well as your flexibility.

Experiments carried out by psychiatrists in the last two decades show that people who can enjoy themselves in a variety of situations have the ability to screen out stimulation and to focus only on what they decide is relevant for the moment. It is this control and deliberateness of attention, as opposed to random overinclusion, that creates a state of enjoyment.

Be aware that increasing your attention and relevance perception abilities, and thereby achieving a high degree of awareness of your experience, involves a shift, which entails, to a certain extent, becoming

146

independent of the social environment. This means you no longer respond exclusively in terms of its social rules, rewards (the immediate gratification of the maximum efficiency illusion), and punishments (e.g., a disappointed supervisor or a missed promotion).

When you achieve this level of autonomy—which requires discipline, perseverance, and willpower—you develop the ability to find enjoyment and purpose, regardless of the circumstances. You now have the freedom to determine the content of your daily experience as it suits you, and you alone.

We have seen in previous chapters how setting a clear goal and paying attention to feedback are keys to effectiveness. To add the element of enjoyment, attention becomes the essential principle.

Becoming Immersed in an Activity

After choosing your purpose, you have to become deeply involved with whatever you are doing. Involvement is greatly facilitated by the ability to concentrate. When attention is carried away constantly, such as by answering messages, you are at the mercy of any stray stimulus that happens to flash by.

Paying Attention to What Is Happening

Concentration leads to involvement, which can only be maintained by constant inputs of attention. Being able to enjoy the moment implies the ability to sustain involvement. This involves a lack of self-consciousness:

147

being concerned about how you are performing a specific task takes attention from the flow of performing the task itself.

You will know when you are on track when you experience a sense of *flow*. Flow has been defined as a condition or feeling of optimal experience[13]; if you pay attention to your own experience, you will notice that this happens when concentration is so intense that there is no attention left over to think about anything irrelevant or to worry about problems. Self-consciousness disappears, and your sense of time becomes distorted. An activity that produces such experience is so gratifying that it becomes detached from results: you do it for its own sake, with little concern for the results that you will get out of it. During flow, you will be completely focusing your attention on the task at hand, thus leaving no room in the mind for irrelevant information, including thoughts. Enjoying life, in essence, involves presence and attention. You will be amazed to find that this is also the time when creative ideas will appear and flow easily.

---

[13] Mihaly Csikszentmihalyi, *Flow: The Psychology of Optimal Experience* (HarperPerennial, 1991).

The Principle of Relevance

Chapter 11 – Snapshot

- One of the basic differences of a person who is able to enjoy each activity he or she pursues it is that it is he or she who has chosen whatever choice the person is pursuing. What he or she does is not random, nor is it the result of outside determining forces.

- Increasing your attention and relevance perception abilities, thereby achieving a high degree of awareness of your experience, involves becoming, to some degree, independent of the social environment so that you no longer respond exclusively in terms of its rewards and punishments.

- Setting a clear goal and paying attention to feedback are keys to effectiveness. To add the element of enjoyment to effectiveness, attention is the most important principle through (1) becoming immersed in an activity and (2) paying attention to what is happening.

- When an activity produces a sense of flow, you do it for its own sake, with little concern about results. You are able to completely focus your attention on the activity, leaving no room in the mind for irrelevant information, including thoughts. Enjoying life, in essence, involves presence and attention.

The Principle of Relevance

EPILOGUE

The Vision

Every breakthrough in science is achieved through a paradigm shifting experience that initially is resisted.

Thomas S. Kuhn, *The Structure of Scientific Revolutions*

An overwhelming quantity of popular new age and spiritual literature points out how the human family is evolving to a new stage, and a new era of deeper awareness is unfolding. Whether to agree with this vision and to what extent is up to the reader's individual belief system and spirituality. Most people would agree, however, that this is a time of profound change, shifting the perceptions we have of our world and the way we interact with each other.

In 1964, Nikolai Kardashev, an astronomer of the former Soviet Union, proposed a method for measuring a civilization's level of technological advancement (commonly referred to as the *Kardashev scale*, which other scientists have, over time, expanded on). The scale categorizes civilizations into three types on the basis of their relationship with and capability to use power sources.

In Kardashev' scale, a civilization is categorized as Type I if it is able to control the energy resources of an entire planet, Type II if it can harness the energy output of its star (solar) system (generating about ten billion times the energy output of a Type I civilization), and Type III if it is able to harnesses the energy output of a galaxy (about ten billion times the energy output of a Type II civilization). A Type I civilization would be able to, for example, control or modify its planet's weather and control the force of other planetary phenomena, such as hurricanes, volcanic eruptions, and earthquakes, transforming them into energy sources. A Type II civilization might be able to funnel the power of solar flares. A Type III civilization would have the resources to colonize a galaxy, extracting energy from the stars forming part of the galaxy, and would have the tools for interdimensional travel.

On the basis of this scale, mankind has not yet evolved to Type I and is still a Type 0 civilization, which relies on dead plants (oil and coal) as a main source of energy. At the average growing rate of about 3 percent per year, our civilization might attain Type I status in about one hundred to two hundred years, Type II status in a few thousand years, and Type III status in about one hundred thousand to one million years.

This theory has undergone some criticism on the basis of the fact that we cannot understand or predict the behavior of advanced civilizations, and therefore Kardashev's theory might be nothing more than a science fiction visualization exercise. Several scientists, however, including

The Principle of Relevance

Michio Kaku, in his work *Hyperspace*, [14] have made reference to Kardashev's work as a very probable, if not precisely measurable, evolutionary pattern.

Kardashev's scale parameter is the ability to use energy resources. Later scientists (such as Carl Edward Sagan, an American astronomer and astrophysicist) suggested that the transition to a higher level on Kardashev's scale could be viewed also in light of a second parameter: the information available to the civilization.

Taking a leap from strictly scientific left-brain thinking and using a bit of imagination and scenario creation, it is not hard to see that the Internet and the information technology revolution are the first visible stages of a transition to a Type I system: a planetary system. Globalization, with all its downsides and problems, is as well.

Another sign of this is the creation of a planetary language. Esperanto, which is an artificially created language, was a first attempt at this. Esperanto did not succeed as hoped by its creators because it is artificially created, and therefore its adoption would require a radical political decision (such as, e.g., the introduction of the euro), which had no reason for being triggered when Esperanto was created. It is, however, starting to become clear to the entire planet the endemic and unstoppable process through which English, through business interaction and the viability of

---

[14] Michio Kaku, *Hyperspace* (Anchor Books, 1995).

The Principle of Relevance

international travel, is naturally and slowly spreading as the common, internationally spoken language.

So are we on the verge of an evolutionary shift to a Type I civilization? What will truly differentiate the new generation of mankind? What will empower mankind as a whole and each individual in his or her own context to take the quantum leap and move to a different level of personal empowerment? Is information availability alone sufficient per se to achieve a new emergence of meaning from the apparent underlying chaos of modern life data overflow?

It should be, at this point, very clear to the reader that I believe the lever to this quantum leap is relevance. Information availability is an energy resource. You need to become apt at using it. The principle of relevance is the key: a subtle refinement of the skill of knowledge working through attention focus and deliberate response—the capacity to take in great quantities of information without being driven to respond automatically to all of it.

Your attention is your most valuable tool. How you use it dictates how you use your time, and how you use your time determines who you are and what you will become.

What will you pay attention to?

The Principle of Relevance

BIBLIOGRAPHY

Note for the reader: This is not meant to be a comprehensive resource list. Its purpose is to be a kick-off reference list of insightful books and materials that will empower and inspire the curious reader with an interest in personal growth and fuel further curiosity toward more research and reading.

Physics and Science

- *Parallel Worlds*, Michio Kaku, Anchor Books, 2005

- *Hyperspace*, Michio Kaku, Anchor Books, 1995

- *The Elegant Universe*, Brian Greene, First Vintage Books, 2000

- *A Brief History of Time*, Stephen Hawkings, Bantam, 1989

- *Complexity: The Emerging Science at the Edge of Order and Chaos*, M. Mitchell Waldrop, Simon and Schuster Paperbacks, 1992

- *Designing for Situation Awareness: An Approach to Human-Centered Design*, M. R. Endsley, B. Bolte, and D. G. Jones, Taylor & Francis, 2003, and *Situation Awareness Analysis and Measurement*, M. R. Endsley and D. J. Garland, (eds.), Lawrence Erlbaum, 2000

Economics

- *Wikinomics*, Don Tapscott and Anthony D. Williams, Portfolio, 2008

Neurolinguistic Programming

- *Introducing NLP*, Joseph O'Connor and John Seymour, Element, 2002

- *The Structure of Magic*, 2 vols., Richard Bandler and John Grinder, Science and Behaviour Books, 1975–1976

Philosophy, Psychology, and Linguistics

- *Relevance: Communication and Cognition*, Dan Sperber and Deirdre Wilson, Blackwell, 1986/1985

- *Flow: The Psychology of Optimal Experience*, Mihaly Csikszentmihalyi, HarperPerennial, 1991

- Alessandro Baricco, *I Barbari (The Barbarians)*, a collection of articles published on "La Repubblica," Feltrinelli, 2008 [*Note: This is a collection of articles written in Italian, and there is not currently a full translation available; however, excerpts of the*

154

work and short video presentations are available on the Internet.]

- "The Roots of Relevance," B. Gorayska and R. O. Lindsay, *Journal of Pragmatics* 19 (1993): 301–23

- "The Magical Number Seven, Plus or Minus Two: Some Limits on Our Capacity for Processing Information," George A. Miller, originally published in *The Psychological Review*, 1956

- *The Structure of Scientific Revolutions*, Thomas S. Kuhn, Chicago Press, 1996

Strategy

- *The Art of War*, Sun Tzu, sixth century B.C., various editions and translations available

- *The Mind Map Book*, Tony Buzan, available at http://www.buzanworld.com

- *The Art of the Long View*, Peter Schwartz, Random House, 1991

Spiritual

- *A New Earth*, Eckhart Tolle, Penguin Books, 2006

Self-Development

- *The 7 Habits of Highly Effective People*, Stephen R. Covey, Fireside, 1990

155

www.ingramcontent.com/pod-product-compliance
Lightning Source LLC
La Vergne TN
LVHW012320060326
832904LV00028B/344